Praise f
Boardro

"When reflecting upon student achievement, along with the culture and climate of a district, one must seek the input of all stakeholders—which brings us to collaborative conversations. Within those conversations a culture is developed, which, as a whole, becomes a *Professional Learning Organization* (PLO). I applaud Dr. Rice for putting this literary resource in perspective as a guide to helping governance teams (School Boards and Superintendents) build PLOs within their districts to help build and maintain student achievement. As a board president and director of special education, I can attest to how shared decision-making leads to student success. I am excited about what impact a PLO systemic approach can have on achievement scores, equity, culture, and community relations for school districts. 'Working with each other instead of around each other builds a strong culture and climate in a community of trust.'"—**Dr. Tamara M. Young, School Board President, Country Club Hills School District 160**

"Dr. Rice is a passionate educational leader with a commitment to changing the landscape of school and district success by providing the steps necessary to reframe thinking about shared ownership for improvement. By defining and recommending the adoption of a *Professional Learning Organization* model, Dr. Rice helps districts apply a new lens through which to view systems change. He invites the reader to recognize the urgency for a shift from individual group responsibility (teachers, administrators, parents, community, etc.) to one of shared accountability. In today's complex educational ecosystem, the stakes have never been higher for the development of a shared mission and vision to meet the challenging social, emotional, and academic needs of all students."—**Dr. Susan Homes, Deputy Director for Professional Development, Illinois Principals Association**

"As he has done in his previous books, *Vanishing School Boards* and *The Essential Quick Flip Reference Guide for School Board Members*, Patrick Rice cuts through the noise that clouds the path to effective public school improvement. His timely roadmap shows school board members how to navigate through today's polarized society and the latest school improvement plans to reclaim their rightful role as elected leaders by working *collaboratively* with all of education's stakeholders. This book is clearly presented, well-researched, and spells out how to get results. It's the one you've been waiting for!"—**Diane M. Cape, Former Director, Education Association**

"Collaborative leadership is essential in the success of any educational institution. In this book, Dr. Rice's continued passion to support effective governing boards and the important role they play in building a culture of improvement is very evident with his emphasis on the implementation of a *Professional Learning Organization* (PLO) model. The content of this book is most certainly beneficial to any public school governing board who strives for success in their school district."—**Cathie Pezanoski, Superintendent, Elwood CCSD #203**

"Dr. Rice has once again explored into the dichotomy between 'it takes a village' and school boards. This book requires school districts to look in the mirror, if they are to achieve at a high level moving forward. The passion behind the book comes through effortlessly and effectively. A must read!"—**Daimon R. Jones Sr., Senior Business Consultant**

"Dr. Patrick Rice has written a timely and most helpful book that should be a choice reading for governance personnel of public schools. As a board member of my local school district, I have been enlightened from the information and approach described in this book. Our District has recently adopted the *Professional Learning Community* concept, and *Equity, From the Boardroom to the Classroom* will be one of the preferred readings. Dr. Rice's book is informative with excellent guiding strategies that define the roles of those contributing to improving student performance and education."—**Nathaniel Anderson, EdD, Former Superintendent, East St. Louis, District 189, School Board Member, Harmony–Emge District 175**

"Dr. Patrick Rice's new book, *Equity, From the Boardroom to the Classroom*, effectively links the *Professional Learning Community* (PLC) Model with a vital stakeholder, the local school board. Typically, the decision makers are many levels removed from the educators—those doing the work with students. Generally, PLCs exist within the schoolhouse but have limited connection with society or the broader community.
"The author offers strategies of inclusion to 'bridge the gap' between the two. For example, Rice discusses systemic collaborative processes for school growth. His book describes the board's capacity and responsibility to collaboratively work with the building's professionals to enact change and build a culture of improvement and growth.
"This author employs his multiple perspectives, linking all the players for success in the classroom, school, district, and region."—**Marleis Trover, PhD, Teacher/Administrator, Public Institution Board Member, Author, and University Instructor**

"*Equity, From the Boardroom to the Classroom* delivers an informative account and perspective of the significant role school boards play in public education. I believe this book will force districts to have courageous conversations surrounding leadership, collaboration, as well as culture and climate. Thank you Dr. Patrick Rice for addressing issues that are far too often overlooked."—**Tammy Nichole Jones, School Board President, Community Consolidated School District 168, Sauk Village**

Equity, From the
Boardroom to the Classroom

Equity, From the Boardroom to the Classroom

Transforming Districts into Professional Learning Organizations

Patrick Rice

ROWMAN & LITTLEFIELD
Lanham • Boulder • New York • London

Published by Rowman & Littlefield
An imprint of The Rowman & Littlefield Publishing Group, Inc.
4501 Forbes Boulevard, Suite 200, Lanham, Maryland 20706
www.rowman.com

6 Tinworth Street, London SE11 5AL, United Kingdom

British Library Cataloguing in Publication Information Available

Library of Congress Cataloging-in-Publication Data Available

ISBN 9781475848670 (cloth: alk. paper) | ISBN 9781475848687 (pbk. : alk. paper) | ISBN 9781475848694 (electronic)

Printed in the United States of America

To my favorite uncle Mr. Harold Justin Sanders (A.K.A. WeeDee),
who always believed and supported me 1,000 percent.
Until we meet again, my beloved uncle and friend.
Love, your nephew Patrick

Contents

Foreword

School board members operate within an evolving framework of governance oversight and with ever-increasing state and federal academic standards that are largely indiscriminate on expectations of compliance. It has become increasingly difficult for board members to determine how they can best be engaged in meaningful contributions to answer the challenges that governance and educational change represent. Dr. Rice's vision represents a timely expansion of professional learning communities (PLCs), the familiar collaborative model utilized by groups of educators to improve teaching skills and students' academic skills.

Dr. Rice's unique extension of that PLC model encourages merging school boards, district staff, and community stakeholders together within a systematic and complementary structure. This merger, working in tandem with district teams, results in a professional learning organization (PLO). PLOs are a logical *next step* for effective school boards actively striving to capitalize and expand upon community engagement with an emphasis on student achievement. Dr. Rice artfully outlines the process, completely adaptable to district size, for successfully implementing and sustaining PLOs as an instrument of cultural change within a district. If you are a board member, this book should definitely be on your reading list, then embraced in the strategic initiatives in your district!

Michael T. Adamson, EdD
Director of Board Services
Indiana School Boards Association
Coauthor of *Building Great School Board–Superintendent Teams:*
A Systematic Approach to Balancing Roles and Responsibilities

Preface

The escalating criticism of public schools and the increasing demands upon educators have led to irreconcilable differences among various stakeholders. This has resulted in reforms concerning how to improve public education, including charter schools, Common Core, the grading of schools, various turnaround models of school reform, unprecedented changes to teacher evaluations and preparation programs, and, more recently, a renewed push toward using vouchers or tax dollars to pay for private school choice. This myriad of expectations has placed our public school system in limbo and in disarray.

The complexity of our public school system, in addition to competing claims and expectations for improvement, has fostered a culture of anarchy. Who are the culprits?

The culprits are hiding in plain sight and include the sheer number of entities that influence the day-to-day operations of schools, teeming from the U.S. and state courts, federal and state laws, U.S. and state departments of education, the U.S. Office of Civil Rights, special interest groups, and some local governing school boards. With so much involvement, authors such as David T. Conley, professor of educational policy and leadership at the University of Oregon, have asked the question, "Who governs our schools?"

In order to improve education for our students, we must unravel this bureaucratic spiderweb and allow for more decisions to be made locally, with some state oversight, as was the intention of the Every Student Succeeds Act (ESSA).

THE NEED FOR COLLABORATIVE LEADERSHIP/GOVERNANCE

Reinvigorating school boards will not make a difference to improve educational outcomes for all students unless school boards practice the concept of "collaborative leadership" and/or "collaborative governance," whereby the school board, staff, students, and community stakeholders can make a difference in addressing educational issues by working together. This mode of governance brings multiple stakeholders together to engage in consensus-oriented decision-making. According to Martin and Rains (2018), "Collaborative leadership is about capitalizing on the strengths and skills of others in the effort to achieve common goals . . . collaborative leadership is about encouraging others to be leaders as well."

According to Ansell and Gash (2007), collaborative governance is defined as "a governing arrangement where one or more public agencies directly engage non-state stakeholders in a collective decision-making process that is formal, consensus-oriented, and deliberative and that aims to make or implement public policy or manage public programs or assets."

School boards must govern by the concept of "collaborative leadership" if they are to be successful. As President Lyndon Johnson noted, "There are no problems we cannot solve together, and very few that we can solve by ourselves." These words of wisdom are of extreme value for school boards, because more and more stakeholders are seeking greater involvement in their districts. Districts that practice collaborative leadership or collaborative governance principles enhance student learning and organizational effectiveness. In this book, collaborative governance refers to both, collaborative governance and collaborative leadership.

A growing number of citizens now believe that today's educational problems are so complex that school boards alone cannot properly solve them without a high level of stakeholder input. In addition, there has been an explosion in the number of citizens questioning the tenets of "participatory democracy," and many are no longer willing to "trust the system" without input and a chance to be actively engaged.

Ansell and Gash (2007) stated that "collaborative governance emerged as a response to the failures of downstream implementation and to the high cost and politicization of regulation. It has developed as an alternative to the adversarialism of interest group pluralism and to the accountability failures of managerialism (especially as the authority of experts is challenged)."

This outlook is shared not only by adults but by our youth as well. In April 2017, a group of 21 young people rallied on the steps of the U.S. Supreme Court as part of an effort to bring a federal suit against President Donald Trump and his administration for failure to hear youth voices regarding global warming. Xiuhtezcatl Martinez, a 16-year-old spokesperson for the group, stated that "not only are the youth going to be inheriting every problem that we see in the world today—after our politicians have been long gone—but our voices have been neglected from the conversation. Our politicians are no longer representing our voices" (Sutter, 2017).

The level of distrust across and between age groups is growing and emerging.

Citizens have a right to engage in lawful protests; nevertheless, some seek involvement in unproductive ways. Regarding local school governance, it is becoming common for citizens to interrupt board meetings or file excessive Freedom of Information Act (FOIA) claims in an attempt to uncover suspected district transgressions. Although collaborative leadership takes time and patience and involves a myriad of people, such collaboration improves the district culture, making such incidents less likely to occur.

POLARIZATION AND THE GOVERNING PROCESS

Nationally, school districts are experiencing a steady increase in the election of agenda-specific board members who choose to represent particular interest groups rather than the larger constituency. Often, these board members refuse to abide by the majority decision of the board and do not believe in the precepts of teamwork.

Perhaps the polarization of politics at the national and state levels has led to a lack of civility in the entire political process. Plus, there is a growing discovery that media and technology can support one's viewpoint. The lack of civility was evidenced by Democratic National Committee chairman Tom Perez in 2017. With children next to him, Perez told an audience in Las Vegas that President Trump "doesn't give a sh-t about health care," in addition to other obscenities concerning Trump's budget proposal (Merica, 2017).

Is there is no longer an incentive to be civil? As DNC chairman, Perez's actions may influence other citizens who seek office under the Democratic umbrella, including those in federal, state, and local elections. For instance, New York Democratic senator Kirsten Gillibrand has used profanity in speeches. In June 2017, Senator Gillibrand used what the media referred to as "F-bombs" during a speech at New York University, lashing out at Trump for not following through with his commitment to improving health care and the tax system for working Americans (Green, 2017).

It is sad when our political leaders are not setting good examples concerning the need for collaboration. Citizens are losing trust in and respect for elected officials to address problems. Many citizens feel their voices are unheard or disregarded. Often this distrust flows downstream from the federal to state to local levels of government. Elected officials who seek to privatize public entities validate critics' concerns that they are unprepared to handle certain public issues and would rather pass the buck (Metzger, 2016).

Many citizens feel the need to become directly involved in areas of governance for constructive change to occur. By utilizing media and technology, citizens can collaborate with other like-minded individuals, and exclude those with whom they dissent, which can impel people to be divided into racial, socioeconomic, religious, generational, and political camps (Desloge, 2017).

This reality, or perception, of government as being out of touch from citizens is apparent in Michigan where top state Republicans indicated a plan to shut down 38 "failing" public schools. The announcement sparked panic, tension, and suspicion from parents and community members. The latter group disagreed with the idea of sending thousands of inner-city students from low-income families to schools some 50 miles away. Citizens were upset because neither their consent nor consideration was taken into account. When leaders utilize the philosophy of "we know what is best for you" without collaboration, it will only fuel distrust and impel people to actively seek to disrupt such a system (Eggert & Williams, 2017).

BENEFITS OF COLLABORATION

Effective boards foster collaboration not only because of the external advantages of getting buy-in from community stakeholders, but also because of internal advantages as well. Effective boards believe in a system where communication and collaboration exist throughout. Boards that create an ambience of collaboration typically experience less staff turnover, better contract negotiations, and significant gains in student achievement.

Teachers welcome collaboration with peers because many teachers are growing tired of working in isolation. According to the *MetLife Survey of the American Teacher* (MetLife, 2009), today's teachers spend an average of 93% of their time working alone, apart from their peers. When teachers are given time to collaborate, student achievement soars. According to DuFour and Eaker (1998), "The most promising strategy for sustained school improvement is developing the ability of school personnel to function as professional learning communities."

The Center for Public Education (CPE, n.d.), an initiative of the National School Boards Association (NSBA), cites eight characteristics of effective school boards. For the fourth characteristic, the CPE states: "Effective school boards have a collaborative relationship with staff and the community and establish a strong communications structure to inform and engage both internal and external stakeholders in setting and achieving district goals."

This characteristic embodies the notion that boards are effective because they obtain various levels of support by directly collaborating with both internal and external stakeholders to promote organizational health and student achievement through venues such as the strategic planning process. The challenge for districts is to determine how to plan and implement a system in which internal and external stakeholders are active participants in the setting and are achieving district goals while not circumventing the superintendent or getting intrusively involved in the day-to-day operations. This book aims to provide such guidance.

PROFESSIONAL LEARNING ORGANIZATION AND THE BOARD ROLE

This book links the board's role to professional learning communities. A professional learning organization refers to the entire "collaborative" district, and within that PLCs are used to departmentalize the organization into manageable systems based on the division of human labor and roles and responsibilities of the work to be completed.

The *strategic* (school board plus superintendent), *tactical* (administration), and *operational* (staff) roles are the three essential professional learning communities (or teams, or departments) that formulate the PLO. PLC refers to the overall name given to the strategic, tactical, and operational learning teams (major district departments) of the district. There are multiple names that could be utilized to describe learning teams that classify under the PLC umbrella based on the three major roles (strategic, tactical, and operational) of the district.

There is a surplus of research on PLCs and teachers, but little that examines how PLCs can be a districtwide model—a PLO—led by the governance team. The aim of this book is to properly inform the governance team (school board and superintendent) how to improve organizational culture by becoming a professional learning organization (PLO), and to explain why becoming a PLO is mutually beneficial for the board, for the superintendent.

This book will also instruct governance teams on driving school improvement districtwide and explain about the role district leadership plays in establishing trust between the district and its schools. A PLO refers to a set of beliefs that the district adheres to by which internal and external stakeholders collaborate to carry out district ends (mission, vision, values, and goals). This includes envisioning how the classroom teacher, administration, and working parents collaborate to address district concerns in exchange for greater organizational efficiency and effectiveness.

This book will illustrate why *PLOs foster equity* for all district students and other stakeholders. Student equity means that all students will have access to the resources they need to ensure their success in meeting educational objectives regardless of race, gender, ethnicity, disability, or socioeconomic status. Districts must describe how to achieve equitable outcomes for all students based on district demographics and resources.

PLOs empower school districts to meticulously monitor key systems through an equity lens that fosters student achievement. Key systems include: wraparound services (e.g., community partnerships), allocation of resources, high-quality educators (e.g., mentoring, induction, peer collaboration, and professional development), how schools are organized to maximize teacher and student learning, student assessments, and student curriculum.

In order to achieve equity for students, districts must ensure that key internal (district staff) and external (parents and community) stakeholders have a voice regarding the educational process of students. In other words, districts must promote collaborative leadership and collaborative governance. When stakeholders do not have a voice, it leads to inequity, which creates organizational tension.

PLOs are unique in that they help to ensure key stakeholders are not excluded from the circle of those who have a vested interest regarding student achievement. A district cannot ensure equity for all students if key decisions are solely based on the ideas and thoughts of select stakeholders (e.g., school board, administrators). As chemist and human rights activist Linus Pauling noted, "The best way to have a good idea is to have lots of ideas." PLOs enable districts to utilize a systems approach of ensuring equity for all students.

This book is not intended to be a deep dive into the intricate details associated with professional learning communities (PLCs), a subcomponent of the PLO. Authors such as DuFour and Eaker have provided a wealth of information related to PLCs. Although insights and an overview are provided regarding the work of PLCs that are subcomponents of the PLO, this book is intended primarily to assist the governance team in understanding its role in a PLO.

A PLO entails supportive and shared leadership, supportive conditions for collective inquiry and learning, and common values and beliefs about improving student learning (Carbaugh, Marzano, & Toth, 2015). As Chrislip and Larson (1994) noted, "It is a shift in the practice of democracy from hostility to civility, from advocacy to engagement, from confrontation to conversation, from debate to dialogue, and from separation to community." A PLO helps look beyond individual interests to collective interests in an attempt to address complex educational issues.

Acknowledgments

First and foremost, I would like to give thanks to my Lord and savior Jesus Christ for all of His blessings and grace. Special thanks to my family, including the love of my life, Crystal, and daughters, Diamond and Emerald. Special thanks to my mom and dad, Reverend Wilkie and Minister Laverne Rice. Special thanks to my siblings: Wilkie, Daryl, William, and Sheila. Special thanks to all of my family members, including the Rice, Sanders, Garretson, and Heard families.

Special thanks to my lifelong best friends Daimon Jones and Leo Smith. And to my special friend that I love so dearly, Monique Rice. Special thanks to my mentees: Isaiah Stevenson, Ronald Madlock, Justin Joslin, and Aulando Sanders (cousin). Special thanks to the Lincoln class of 1993 and my mentors Dr. Freddie A. Banks, Dr. Nate Anderson, Dr. Nick Osborne, and Dr. Dick Robinson. Special thanks to all of my former teachers, specifically Mrs. Laura Redmond and the late Mrs. Muriel Harris.

Special thanks to the numerous professionals who aided me in the creation of this book, including Gary Adkins, Theresa Kelly Gegen, Diane Cape, Jenny Harkins, Reatha Owen, Prof. Harry Mosley, Jeffery Campbell, Dr. Kevin Settle, Shelly Kuhns and Altamont Community Unit 10 Schools, Dr. Nate Cunningham, Dr. Jim Rosborg, Dr. David Bartz, Mrs. D'Karla Assagai, Dr. Elizabeth Reynolds, Mr. John Perez and Calumet SD 132 board members/administration, Ms. Jean Chrostoski, Ms. Cathie Pezanoski, Mrs. Emeka Jackson-Hicks (mayor of East St. Louis), Minister Ralph Muhammad (Muhammad's Mosque 28B), Mr. Michael Hubbard, Mr. Anthony and Georgina Veshusio, Dr. Sue Homes, the staff of the Illinois Association of School Boards, my former staff at J. L. Buford Intermediate Center, and to the members of the Black Educational Advocacy Coalition (BEAC).

    Special thanks to my lifetime pastor, Dr. Norman E. Owens, and to his late wife, Charlotte. Special thanks also to my church, Pavey Chapel C. M. E. Church. Also, special thanks to the oldest and coldest fraternity in which I am a member, Alpha Phi Alpha Fraternity, Inc.

Introduction

No organization can outperform its leadership, so the board must play the key role in transforming the district's culture. The board is ultimately responsible for the oversight of the district, including the selection of the superintendent to carry out the day-to-day operations. As psychologist Robert Evans noted, "Major change almost never wells up from the bottom. It begins near the top (and if not, it almost never takes hold without strong backing from the top). It typically starts with a key leader and a small core of people who care strongly about a particular solution to a problem. It spreads out from there" (as cited in DuFour, DuFour, & Eaker, 2008).

The board must be clear about its expectations and codify them in board policies and administrative procedures. If a board expects its district to have systems in place to ensure systemic collaboration as with PLO models, this must be communicated, expected, and monitored. As English writer Lewis Carroll noted, "If you don't know where you are going, any road will get you there."

To foster a collaborative culture, boards must display "thermostat leadership" as opposed to "thermometer leadership." "Thermostat leadership" is practiced when the board is actively involved in setting, maintaining, or adjusting district culture in order to ensure alignment with district priorities. Comparatively, "thermometer leadership" is used when a board governs by a laissez-faire approach and seeks to mandate a specific culture without becomingly actively involved.

Although the board is ultimately responsible for the oversight of the district, effective boards must share the authority and empower the superintendent to act on their behalf to help build such a culture. Therefore, the selection of the superintendent is one of the most important decisions the board will make in building a culture based on the precepts of collaborative leadership. John Carver (2001), creator of policy governance, noted that "authority not given away does little good, but too much given away constitutes rubber stamping or dereliction. How can the board have its arms around the system without its fingers in it?"

This book will provide information about how the board can govern by the concept of "informed leadership" to ensure a proper balance between the sharing of such authority.

A PLO IS NOT ANOTHER COME-AND-GO REFORM

In an effort to bolster student achievement, districts have bought into various ideologies, such as top-down governance, merit pay, and a variety of turnaround models. This was the case for Shawnee High School in Louisville, Kentucky. After 3 years, a $1.5 million investment, staffing turnarounds, content-area specialists, guidance from a veteran educator, and support from state and federal departments of education, there was no significant academic progress made at Shawnee (Klein, 2013).

Collaboration is not a onetime strategy to reach a goal; rather, it must be a way of life for the district, or the district's way to address educational concerns utilizing systems, and not a program the district purchases. A PLO is a pragmatic approach based on the view that Chrislip and Larson (1994) noted when they stated, "There is a belief that if you bring the appropriate people together in constructive ways with good information, they will create authentic visions and strategies for addressing the shared concerns of the organization or community."

In this view, leaders are not those who are more adept in solving common issues but instead are the ones who are able to gather the appropriate people to develop better visions and alternative ways to solve common concerns. As former president Woodrow Wilson noted, "We should not only use all the brains we have, but all that we can borrow."

Research is clear: No school reform aimed at improving student learning will be successful without strong leadership and support from the governance team as well as the belief in shared decision-making. The key to improving learning must be a systemic process that is grounded in collaboration among various stakeholders. Without leadership, support, and collaboration, it is doubtful that a school reform will be successful, regardless of how effective the reform may appear.

When districts invest in the concept of becoming a PLO, they can get off the pendulum swing of ushering in new educational reforms while refusing to buy the canned educational solutions of snake oil salesmen. PLO districts understand that the organization as a collective unit can solve an array of problems because individual talents and skills are harnessed in a group effort to meet organizational goals. This requires that individuals in the organization are aware of each other's skill sets and contributions to the organization. As Sun Tzu, the Chinese military general and strategist, once said, "Know your enemy and know yourself and you can fight a hundred battles without disaster."

Governance teams must strive to build a culture in which all stakeholders know how they contribute individually and collectively to accomplish district ends and have buy-in regarding the process. When governance teams create this level of synergy and understand the ins and outs of their organization, the district can overcome the complex challenges of increasing student achievement without disaster, whether it comes to meeting Every Student Succeeds Act (ESSA) provisions or the Program for International Student Assessment (PISA) standards, or some other learning initiative.

AUDIENCE

This book is geared to various audiences, but specifically toward the governance team, because it provides the key leadership to ensure that a district is operating systemically as a PLO. This book seeks to inform the governance team of the various benefits of becoming a PLO, such as enhancing board and superintendent relationships, developing a sense of ownership and pride in the district from the district stakeholders, reducing staff turnover, creating "win-win" collective bargaining agreements, and fostering and sustaining student achievement.

School board members will understand how to properly transform district culture to maximize student learning and organizational effectiveness without engaging in micromanagement. School boards will learn how PLOs can ensure that the board is properly informed of district activities, which allows the board to become more adept in making data-informed decisions.

This book will explain why it is in the best interest of the superintendent to form a districtwide PLO. Superintendents will not be successful without having a thorough understanding of the district's operations and intricate knowledge of the day-to-day issues of the organization. By following the tenets of a PLO, the superintendent will possess and understand this information. This information not only allows the superintendent to properly inform the board of district affairs, but to properly forecast future district needs as well. Furthermore, this sends a message to staff that the superintendent is not the individual with all of the solutions to district problems, but rather that he or she is role-modeling the concept that, through collaboration, district problems can be solved together, which will create districtwide synergy.

Principals, teachers, and other staff members will understand how the power of becoming a PLO can provide an increase in job satisfaction, as well as a sense of ownership, and they will discover how working collectively as a team can provide systems of support and significant gains in meeting professional and collective goals. Moreover, staff members can understand how the district is interconnected. This will enable these staff members to have a better perspective and appreciation for the governance aspects of their district.

This book will be helpful to educational professors and various educational associations because it provides a unique frame to illustrate how districts can be governed by utilizing the concepts of collaborative leadership and collaborative governance. These educational leaders must always reinvigorate our approaches to school management and governance, as well as bear responsibility to teach prospective, current, and future leaders about new and innovative practices concerning our craft.

Finally, this book will enable citizens and other community stakeholders to envision how the district forms a collaborative relationship with the staff and community, through effective communications in the setting and achieving of district goals based on mutual interest. And it should provide an understanding that the governance team ultimately makes decisions on behalf of the community but does so only after stakeholder voices are genuinely considered.

BOOK ORGANIZATION

This book will explain why school districts must govern as PLOs. Top-down management practices are a relic of the past and are unproductive in building and fostering a culture wherein student achievement can flourish.

Chapter 1 explores the importance of organizational culture and explains who is responsible for building organizational culture, the need for collaboration and teamwork, and the need for a happy medium between top-down and bottom-up leadership.

Chapter 2 defines the concept of a PLO and PLCs. This chapter will give a brief historical overview of the models and the various components that comprise a PLO, including the key concepts of focus on learning, focus on results, and focus on collaboration. Chapter 3 examines each of the various PLC teams as well as a discussion concerning the effective norms and components (strategic, tactical, and operational) of a PLO and PLCs. The chapter also discusses the importance of governance team (school board and superintendent) buy-in, learning team norms, and the orientation of board members and staff regarding district expectations.

Chapter 4 examines why it is essential for the governance team to govern using the concept of "informed oversight" and why the governance team should insist upon the triangulation of data. The chapter further discusses how the governance team can effectively monitor PLOs, including PLC reports, stakeholder surveys, and/or focus groups, and the need to conduct exit interviews of individuals leaving the district.

Chapter 5 discusses the advantages of becoming a PLO, including the positive impact it has on board–superintendent relationships, as well as explaining how a PLO benefits students, staff, and parents. Chapter 6 discusses the role community engagement plays in enhancing a school district's organizational culture.

Chapter 7 discusses the implementation stages of becoming a PLO, including the need for cultural audits and/or district continuum assessment surveys to monitor the success of beginning and sustaining a PLO culture. Chapter 8 discusses the importance of school board and superintendent leadership.

Chapter 9 makes a final case why districts should readily adopt the PLO model, including a look at similar models such as the kaizen continuous improvement model. Chapter 9 also discusses how PLOs can adapt to district size and meet state and federal guidelines and standards. Chapter 10 summarizes the book based upon the insights of a leading educational scholar.

Chapter One

Why Organizational Culture Matters

Every organization has an organizational culture, whether it is a 7-Eleven with a handful of employees or the U.S. military with thousands of servicemen and women. School districts are no different. The culture, like a garden, must be tended to in order to have a great yield. What is organizational culture? The term refers to the quality and character of the organization based upon various stakeholders' views of the organization. Elements of organizational culture in a school district include safety, relationships, and the condition of the teaching and learning environment.

According to Psychology and Society (n.d.), organizational culture reflects the values, beliefs, and norms that characterize an organization as a whole. Values reflect what the organization feels is important, beliefs entail how goals should be met, and norms reflect the accepted behaviors of the organization. Values, beliefs, and norms all serve as guiding principles for the organization (Psychology and Society, n.d.). The organizational culture refers to the more visible policies, procedures, practices, procedures, and routines that govern the organization, as well as its behavioral expectations and reward structure. Culture is the personality of the organization.

To visualize the cultural values, beliefs, and norms present in an organization, imagine visiting your local library. What values and norms are present? More simply, how are people expected to behave? Concerning values, most people typically view the library as a place where learning is not restricted to certain classes, but rather everyone has an opportunity to learn. The library also serves as a learning community for various individuals and groups.

Regarding behavioral expectations, people are expected to adhere to various norms when visiting a library. Norms such as the "quiet, please" rule help to ensure that everyone can experience a learning environment free from

1

unwanted distractions. There are other norms as well, such as not damaging or destroying library property, no eating and/or drinking, no smoking, and no dress-code violations.

If someone disregarded library rules, such as no listening to loud music, imagine the response of people inside the library community. How would such an individual be perceived, and would the social norms at the library motivate the individual to adjust his or her behavior to meet those established norms? Wouldn't you agree that a person who broke library rules by playing loud music would be asked to leave if he or she did not comply? Library rule breakers will either conform to library expectations or exit library premises, in part due to the powerful library culture of ensuring that no one is distracting others from learning.

Imagine if this same individual claimed a right to listen to loud music and believed that he or she were being treated unfairly. Would commonsense people rally to support this person's cause? No, because people would protect and nourish healthy library cultural norms aimed to ensure a safe and orderly learning environment. This cultural expectation is based upon the needs of the learning community in its many quests, including finding jobs, starting businesses, and locating resources related to personal and professional interests. In addition, people generally feel a sense of collective ownership of their local libraries.

Comparatively, if healthy social norms—strong systemic collaboration, communication, and a sense of collective ownership among various district stakeholders—were present in a school district, wouldn't it be challenging for any stakeholder to go against these established district norms? It is logical to assume people will generally conform to cultural expectations if expectations are shared and agreed upon by the vast majority. Admittedly, there may be some anomalies, but commonsense thinking suggests that collaboration will be more effective in obtaining stakeholder buy-in, especially when compared to not involving stakeholders at all.

BENEFITS OF A PLO DISTRICT

In PLO districts where various stakeholders, such as administrators, board members, parents, students, teachers, and others, frequently spend time and collaborate, there is a natural propensity to develop a common set of expectations. These expectations evolve into systems of written and unwritten rules, to which individuals adhere in order to stay in good standing with one another. As a result of these expectations, it would be challenging for stakeholders to bash or not to support the interests of the district because expectations were collaboratively shared and agreed upon (Gruenert, 2008). The payoff of such collaboration is providing *equity* as well as ensuring that all students learn at high levels, which should be inherent goals of all districts.

Teachers find it difficult to work independently from other teachers in collaborative systems. This includes beginning teachers who have their own ideas about effective teaching based on their recent educational experiences. If those experiences are not shared by the group, teachers will be apt to assimilate if they desire to be a part of the school's culture (Gruenert, 2008).

Collaboration between governance teams and teachers will minimize the "us-versus-them" mentality between the two. Attorney Brandon Wright with the Miller, Tracy, Braun, Funk & Miller, Ltd. law firm in Illinois stated that when there is a high degree of collaboration between the governance team and teachers, districts experience fewer tumultuous problems and better contract negotiations (B. Wright, personal communication, October 18, 2017).

Besides teachers, school board members in a collaborative system will also be motivated to operate as a team as well because of the internal pressures to work together. School board members are more likely to abide by the majority decision and to continue fostering group goals, as compared to individual agendas, due to the power that collaborative leadership yields.

How the Board Impacts Culture

When attention is given to the overall culture of the district, the culture advertently and/or inadvertently impacts the district's climate or the collective mood or attitude of the organization. Whose job ultimately is it to build and monitor the organizational culture based on the district's priorities or ends (values and beliefs, mission, vision, goals)? Although the superintendent plays a key role as the person responsible for the day-to-day operations of the district, it is ultimately the board's responsibility.

Board members are the only elected officials whose sole purpose is to serve as trustees on behalf of the community to ensure that district schools represent the values of the community. Similar to President Lincoln's Gettysburg Address concerning representative democracy, we need to ensure the survival of local control in our public schools: that school district ends (mission, vision, goals) are formulated of the people, by the people, and for the people, by way of a locally elected school board.

In utilizing the concepts of "collaborative governance" through venues as PLOs, governance teams must realize that no two PLO districts will look exactly the same. Why? Because a district's culture should be unique and represent the values of the community it serves. The culture is not confined to a particular building or school, but again it represents the attitude of the organization.

The task for the governance team members is to determine how they would like to best use human capital in the organization to ensure systemic collaboration and communication to best meet and/or address organizational goals and/or concerns. Like past failed reforms, if organizations try cookie-cutter models of reform without regard to who they are and do not solicit stakeholder input, as Sun Tzu noted in *The Art of War*, the result will be disastrous (Tzu, 1994).

To successfully and positively influence district culture by becoming a PLO, districts need to adhere to the words of author, orator, and presidential advisor Booker T. Washington, who said, "Cast down your bucket, where you are." Districts must cast down their buckets where they are, seeking to build and sustain a collaborative culture by first examining and using existing human capital within the organization primarily to ensure that all students learn at high levels.

How the Superintendent Impacts Culture

Although the board's role in a PLO is to help establish the direction of the district, the board must rely on the superintendent's expertise to bring this vision into reality. To ensure a good working relationship, the board and superintendent must agree regarding the direction of the district and the philosophy of "collaborative governance" if the district is to become successful in becoming a PLO. According to Peter Senge (1990), this requires the superintendent to assume the role of a gardener to meet the expectations of the board.

Similar to a gardener, the superintendent needs to study the environment—the garden—and understand his or her responsibility to the environment, communicate and describe the purpose of the garden/organization, have a plan to grow or enhance it, ensure that the right people—or plants—are in place, and nurture individuals to help them produce. Like a good gardener, the superintendent's primary objective is to determine the conditions that stimulate stakeholder growth (e.g., focusing and prioritization of work—pruning) in the garden/organization, as well as determine what conditions could hinder stakeholder growth.

Superintendents who do not believe in "collaborative governance" principles but instead manage people by using top-down management techniques will not experience continuous systemic success. Top-down leaders too often rely on intimidation to pressure people to develop more quickly. Superintendents in a PLO must adhere to the African proverb that states, "Grass does not grow faster if you pull it." Futile attempts to make grass grow by pulling its blades will only kill the grass. Superintendents in a PLO are servant leaders and are concerned about how to build intrinsic motivation. These servant leaders encourage individuals to grow by relying on encouragement and training (Senge, 1990).

Building and sustaining an effective organizational culture doesn't happen overnight. It takes time to develop and maintain a healthy organizational culture. The process starts with the board being certain about what it wants, which will enable the board to monitor progress and compliance about its expectations. Chapter 2 takes a closer look at PLOs and how they can best assist the governance team in building a collaborative culture.

Chapter Two

A Look at PLOs

The purpose of school boards can be summed up in one word—governance. School boards govern or "oversee" district operations through the policies they enact. School boards have a legal authority to govern the district on behalf of their community. According to the Illinois Association of School Boards' (IASB) Foundational Principles of Effective Governance, the primary governing task of school boards is to clarify the district's purpose by defining and articulating district ends (core values/beliefs, mission, vision, and goals). Ends focus on student learning and on organizational effectiveness (IASB, 2017).

Ends define the purpose of the organization and provide clarity to the staff regarding their day-to-day duties. District ends are essential, since they unite the entire organization with a common purpose or sense of direction. Once ends are established, it is the job of the school board to monitor and to ensure that district ends are being carried out with fidelity. As former president Ronald Reagan said, "Surround yourself with the best people you can find, delegate authority, and don't interfere as long as the policy you've decided upon is being carried out."

District ends create clarity for the organization because they address important questions, such as: "Why do we exist?" "How do we behave?" "What business are we in?" "How will success be defined?" "What are our current priorities?" "And who must do what and when?" In short, ends help ensure that members of the organization are all pulling in the same direction. Without a clear vision or direction, the organization is purposeless. Dissatisfaction and discouragement are the fruits of organizations without vision. As leadership expert John C. Maxwell (2001) noted, "Great vision precedes great achievement."

Once the district has clarity, it must continuously invest in human capital to reinforce district priorities.

To accomplish organizational goals and objectives, PLO districts are primarily concerned about the arrangement of human (staff) systems that enhance student learning and organizational effectiveness. The governance team relies on the feedback from these human systems to monitor organizational effectiveness and to ensure that its purpose (district ends) is being fulfilled.

THREE BIG IDEAS OF A PLO

PLO districts are guided by three big ideas associated with student learning and organizational effectiveness. (Carbaugh et al., 2015; DuFour & Eaker, 1998) identify these three big ideas of a PLO; the language is similar for PLCs:

- *Focus on learning*
- *Focus on results*
- *Focus on collaboration*

A focus on learning entails what students should know and be able to do, and what assistance will be provided to students who have learning difficulties. The mantra of PLO districts is the belief that all students will achieve at high levels. A focus on learning is essential considering this is one of the primary missions of public schools and for the continued success of our democracy. Scott Turow (2011), U.S. writer and lawyer, once said, "Widespread public access to knowledge, like public education, is one of the pillars of our democracy, a guarantee that we can maintain a well-informed citizenry." Thomas Jefferson also said, "Wherever the people are well-informed they can be trusted with their own government."

A focus on results encompasses how district expectations (district goals) are being monitored, access to meaningful data, how issues are resolved, and how the district celebrates its success. As this book will later discuss, in a PLO the school board is not totally dependent on the superintendent for information regarding the monitoring of outcomes related to district expectations. Monitoring is a vital component of PLO districts because monitoring allows the organization to evaluate its effectiveness in obtaining organizational outcomes. As the old cliché states, "What gets measured, gets done."

A focus on collaboration entails how systemic collaboration and communication are fostered throughout the district to ensure organizational effectiveness (Carbaugh et al., 2015). PLO districts require teamwork to carry out organizational aims. The district has to be thoughtful regarding how human capital is utilized and how systems are structured to maximize systemic collaboration and communication.

Similar to chess, the movement of human capital can significantly alter the organization for better or worse, such as placing people in the wrong positions, and stifling creativity and personal satisfaction by not having mechanisms in place to hear the voices of the district's stakeholders. Once effective mechanisms are in place, the district must not lose focus in promoting the continued success of these systems.

Choosing to become a PLO is a wise move for school boards since many boards struggle with how they are impacting student learning, monitoring organizational outcomes, and ensuring staff collaboration regarding the direction of the district. More importantly, a PLO allows boards to have a greater impact regarding how the school board can play an intrinsic role in creating the conditions for learning to occur, which includes the aforementioned (monitoring and collaboration).

Out of the three big ideas of PLO districts, school boards in non-PLO districts experience difficulty monitoring organizational operations. This includes when it may be appropriate and/or vital for the school board to hear from other district staff members regarding district ends and other key decisions. Figure 2.1 below is an example of a traditional or formal organizational model that school boards typically rely on to monitor student learning and organizational effectiveness.

A common practice for effective superintendents is to allow central office administrators and building administrators to provide various reports to the board for sundry reasons; often this practice is not culturally embedded in the operational norms of the district. The failure to monitor district ends in non-PLO districts may be due to a variety of reasons. Frequently, no strategic plan is in place, data that the board needs to properly monitor organizational objectives is missing, the frequency with which data should be monitored is

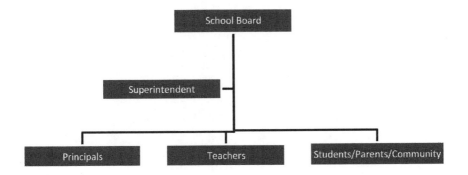

Figure 2.1. Traditional governance model

undermined, and how to properly evaluate the superintendent in meeting district goals is uncertain.

To properly monitor the outcomes of the organization in a PLO, including systemic collaboration and ensuring equity throughout the organization, the school board hears from a variety of key staff members (e.g., department heads, teacher leaders). Figure 2.2 below is an example of a PLO organizational model that will be discussed later that allows school boards to monitor student learning and organizational effectiveness based in part on direct input from multiple stakeholders.

Receiving updates from various staff members allows the school board to be better informed of the day-to-day operations of the organization while not circumventing the authority of the superintendent, since these reports are orchestrated by the superintendent. The superintendent, in the role as the chief administrator of the district, arranges for key personnel to update the school board, which benefits both the school board and the superintendent. This process of governance is called "informed oversight," which will be discussed in detail in Chapter 6.

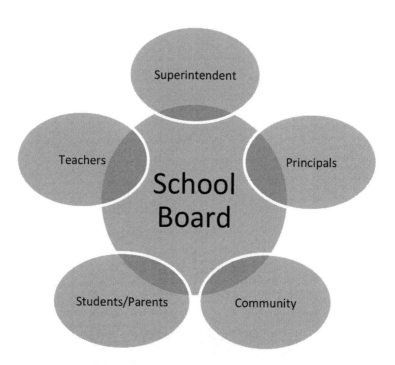

Figure 2.2. PLO governance organizational model

Board president Shelly Kuhns of Altamont Community Unit 10 Schools in Illinois discussed the importance of the board being properly informed when she noted:

> As a school board, our role is to make good decisions and provide direction for the district. Good decisions are based on good information. Information needs to be bidirectional. Although the superintendent works closely with all department leaders to ensure the district goals are addressed, the board needs to maintain open communication with department leaders to ensure systemic collaboration. District strategic planning requires clear information on the strengths and weaknesses within each area. Despite everyone's best efforts, information is lost or distorted when passed through layers, so it is helpful to communicate directly with the department leaders periodically. The superintendent can facilitate the communication of the board with each department at timely intervals and at a frequency most helpful for each department (annually, semi-annually, or quarterly). Not only does this provide effective bidirectional communication, it facilitates succession planning when the time comes for replacement of key positions in the district. For example, in our district we anticipate the retirement of our superintendent within the next 2–3 years. Establishing clear bidirectional communication with department leaders contributes to successful succession planning. (S. Kuhns, personal communication, July 30, 2017)

School boards that lack the expertise of properly monitoring organizational effectiveness or governing effectively often utilize a "hands-off" approach or have attempted to engage in micromanagement of the superintendent (Alsbury & Gore, 2015). Board micromanagement of the superintendent typically leads to superintendent turnover, which leads to an inconsistency in implementing district objectives as well as a negative impact on staff morale.

PLO districts are unique in that they are structured in a way that allows the school board to guide effectively, to monitor, and to understand the overall operations of the district without micromanaging, and/or by using a more balanced governance approach (a board that is neither disengaged nor engaged in micromanagement of the superintendent) as noted by Alsbury and Gore (2015).

As John Carver (2001), policy governance expert, asked, "How can the board have its arms responsibly around the organization without micromanaging or being directly involved in the day-to-day operations of the district?"

PLOs are districts that believe and practice the precepts of "collaborative governance" and "systems theory." As noted, this requires the district to pay attention to how systems and/or human capital are structured in ways that enable the organization to be efficient by having a shared purpose through systemic collaboration and communication. Leaders in such an organization believe as Ray Kroc, founder of McDonald's, eloquently stated, "No one of us is more important than the rest of us" (Maxwell, 2001).

To bring this vision into reality, PLOs consistently monitor and evaluate how internal and external stakeholders collaborate and communicate to accomplish district ends. This requires intentional linkage, especially between the school district and its schools (Van Clay, Soldwedel, & Many, 2011). Traditionally, school turnaround models have failed to bring about systemic change because of issues related to public bureaucracy, such as focusing on rules and complying with procedures rather than outcomes and an unwillingness and/or unresponsiveness to adapting to external needs (Bimber, 1993; Cunningham, 2016).

EXAMINING THE ROLE OF PLCS

The link (how internal stakeholders collaborate) is established by dividing human capital into collaborative teams or professional learning communities (PLCs) throughout the system. This entails supportive and shared leadership, supportive conditions for collective inquiry and learning, and common values and beliefs about improving student learning. PLC teams communicate and collaborate with one another to enhance synergy throughout the organization.

Since organizations can range from small to large with various divisions of labor, PLCs are used in PLOs to departmentalize the organization into manageable systems. By departmentalizing the organization, the key work of the organization is divided based on the nature and responsibility of work to be completed. This allows for increased innovation, as staff can thus have a more direct impact regarding their work in the organization.

Without departments, key decisions may be more centralized at the governance or management level, resulting in top-down management carrying out the aims of the organization. PLO districts realize that top-down leadership seldom results in staff buy-in since direction is solely provided from the top; with no buy-in from other stakeholders, there is no sense of "shared purpose."

PLCs are simply the various interconnected components or organizational departments that compose the PLO to carry out the organization's mission. All organizations, regardless of their size, need some sort of organizational structure to operate properly. Without structure, the organization cannot be successful in operating efficiently, nor in ensuring that stakeholders' voices will be heard at the appropriate level associated with their role with the organization.

In his book *Leading for Learning* (2009), Phillip C. Schlechty described the difference between a "learning community" and "learning organization." He noted how the learning organization simply legitimizes the learning community or communities such as PLCs. He noted that learning organizations are formal social organizations that purposefully create, support, and use learning communities and communities of learners as the primary means of inducting new members; creating, developing, importing, and exporting knowledge; assigning tasks and evaluating performances; and establishing goals and maintaining direction. Learning organizations create and maintain networks of learning communities and use these networks as the primary means by which the work of the organization is accomplished.

In short, a PLO is simply a systemic organizational structure grounded in districtwide alignment of goals through ongoing collaboration between its internal and external stakeholders. Using a compass analogy, understanding true north helps a traveler navigate more accurately by understanding his or her position relative to the North Pole (Van Clay et al., 2011). Similarly, aligning the activities of individuals in a district allows members to stay on course toward reaching common goals by understanding their role or position relative to the district's true north or overall district ends (values/beliefs, mission, vision, goals).

In a PLO, who decides what true north is? The governance team (school board and superintendent) determines the district's true north but relies on stakeholder input to determine what true north is. Soliciting stakeholder input (collaborative governance) is one way the governance team help keeps the "public" in public schools by detecting what the community values and expects from its schools.

When district systems are aligned and are interdependent, outcomes are more predictable and are more easily attained. Moreover, change in one part of the system will inevitably affect other parts of the system in carrying out district ends. If systems are not properly aligned or operating in mutually supportive and interconnected ways, the organization would not be efficient and effective in accomplishing any of its goals, nor its primary goal of increasing student achievement.

As Chubb and Moe (1990) noted, "All things being equal, a student in an effectively organized school achieves at least a half-year more than a student in an ineffectively organized school over the last two years of high school." Chubb and Moe (1990) believed that excessive bureaucracy that stems from politics is the primary cause of concern for most schools because it leads to top-down hierarchical management systems, which inevitably promote conflict. It is my experience that excessive bureaucracy has motivated districts to try multiple reform initiatives, resulting in a lack of focus on what the district priorities are.

In order to establish and maintain a functional PLO system, there must be a high degree of trust throughout the organization. Staff members must genuinely believe that their voices matter and that the administration and school board are sincere in their efforts to create synergy based on the precepts of "collaborative governance." On the other hand, staff members must understand that the school board makes all final decisions regarding district ends but genuinely solicits and seeks to incorporate the views of various stakeholders when making organizational decisions. This approach can best be summed up by stating that "staff is allowed to have a say, but not necessarily can they have it their way."

History of PLCs

The term *professional learning community* (or PLC) emerged among researchers as early as the 1960s, when they offered the concept as an alternative to the isolation in which most teachers worked. In addition, traditional public school principals were not expected to be instructional experts and, as a result, teachers were not given appropriate support. Traditionally, it was quite common for beginning teachers to receive only a classroom book, a schedule, and a list of their extracurricular duties. This reality led teachers to think creatively as to how they could support one another, which was later tokened PLCs (Honawar, 2008).

The term *PLC* is attributed to Shirley Hord (1997), having been coined with her work with the Southwest Educational Development Laboratory (SEDL). Ironically, research suggests that a majority of teachers still work in isolation from their peers and seldom receive effective mentoring (National Council on Teacher Quality, 2017).

PLCs have evolved to refer to a system of supportive and shared leadership and supportive conditions for collective learning. Attributes include supportive and shared leadership, collective inquiry, common shared values and beliefs, and supportive conditions for collective learning. As previously noted, PLCs are focused on three big ideas: a focus on learning (students should know and be able to do), results (what data should be reviewed and how often), and collaboration (team members have an opportunity to communicate and collaborate with one another) (Carbaugh et al., 2015; DuFour & Eaker, 1998).

Much credit is given to educational practitioners DuFour and Eaker, who helped to revolutionize the work of PLCs and to popularize the term. DuFour and Eaker founded a company named Solution Tree for the purposes of helping districts implement PLCs. Many educators look to Solution Tree for resources and other types of guidance in establishing PLCs.

Dufour's hands-on experience with PLCs originated when he was a principal at Adlai E. Stevenson High School and assisted the school in becoming a PLC. During this time, the school became one of the first in the nation to embrace what are known today as professional learning communities. Since becoming a PLC, the school has received many accolades for advancing student achievement (Carbaugh et al., 2015).

It should be noted that many educational pundits classify PLCs as solely representing teacher collaboration, in which teachers work together as professionals to bolster student learning as they share collective responsibility for student learning. This includes addressing common issues as compared to buying and/or implementing "canned turnaround models" of school reform, which are seldom, if ever, successful. As this book describes, PLCs are composed of various learning communities inside the PLO organization.

Three Key PLC Components

The strategic, tactical, and operational roles are present in all school districts (Van Clay et al., 2011). As noted, it is important to keep in mind that the entire "collaborative" district is referred to as a PLO. Additionally, PLCs are used to departmentalize the organization into manageable systems based on the division of human labor and their role and responsibility regarding the work to be completed. The strategic (school board plus superintendent), tactical (administration), and operational (staff) roles are the three essential PLC learning communities (or learning teams or departments) that formulate the PLO.

It must also be remembered that the name *PLO* refers to the entire "collaborative" organization. Moreover, the name *PLC* refers to the overall name given to the strategic, tactical, and operational learning teams of the district. There are multiple names that could be utilized to describe learning teams that classify under the PLC umbrella based on the three major roles (strategic, tactical, and operational) of the district. For instance, the governance team deals with the district's strategic role, whereas the teacher learning team deals with the district's operational role. Chapter 3 describes other possible district PLC teams.

The PLO is led by the strategic (governance) team, which is composed of elected/appointed school board members. These members represent the governing branch of the organization. The superintendent who oversees the day-to-day operations of the district and is the chief administrator of the district is also a de facto member of the strategic team. The strategic team has an obligation to ensure student learning and organization effectiveness, and to serve as a conduit to ensure two-way conversations with the community; this team sits in trust for or ensures the community has a voice in the direction (district ends) of its schools.

The tactical team of the PLO represents the district's administrative leaders (e.g., assistant superintendents, principals, special education director). The tactical team is led by the superintendent, who is the chief administrative official for the district. This team influences staff performance by devising an operational plan as to how the organization can best meet organizational goals. The operational team represents the general staff of the organization, which carries out the overall aims of the organization. The staff represents "the boots on the ground" in carrying out the mission of the organization.

The strategic, tactical, and operational teams all play vital roles in the success of the organization. Using home construction as an analogy, the strategic team or homeowners decide how they would like a particular house constructed. Let's suppose that the homeowners (strategic/board) have to follow or meet certain expectations of a homeowners association (general community), which has the legal authority to enforce rules and regulations (the community's right to elect school board members) that focus on restrictions and building and safety issues (community expectations concerning district priorities).

To construct this house, the homeowners must lay out a vision for what the house should look like, as the district's strategic team answers the question regarding the overall purpose of the school district. If the homeowners fail to communicate their goals, they have abnegated their responsibility, just as a school board would by not clarifying the district's purpose. Therefore, one of the first orders of business for becoming a PLO district is for the governance team to clarify the district's purpose by formulating district ends. District ends should be formulated in concert with both internal and external stakeholders.

Once the homeowner (strategic/board) provides direction, the contractor (tactical/administrative) designs the blueprint and identifies what resources are needed to carry out the homeowner expectations (district ends). Strong communication must exist to ensure that the home (district) is being constructed or implemented with fidelity. This includes the contractor informing the homeowners of project updates, just as the superintendent advises the board how goals are being carried out according to its vision and guidelines. It includes reporting how the organization is in compliance with building codes for the house, just as the state, federal, and other legal statutes govern the operations of the school district.

To properly inform the homeowners (strategic/board) about progress and to ensure that work is being performed to their expectations, the contractor (tactical/superintendent) may allow key workers (operational/staff) to provide updates to the homeowners (strategic/board) as well. This further adds to the contractor's (superintendent's) credibility and reassures the homeowners that the job is being completed. By hearing from other key personnel, the homeowners (strategic/board) trust the contractor (tactical/administration), but trust is enhanced through verification.

Because the tactical (administration) and operational (staff) teams are composed of experts regarding their trades, the homeowners (strategic/board) must rely on the contractor's (superintendent's) skills and recommendations to oversee the day-to-day operations of building the house (daily activities of the district). The homeowners (tactical/board) provide indirect guidance to the workers (operational/staff) that actually build the house (implementation of district goals).

Given this analogy, if the strategic, tactical, and operational teams all understand their roles and duties, including how the teams are interconnected, and all are given opportunities to engage in meaningful collaboration and communication regarding the construction of the house (direction of the district), then the end result would ultimately be the successful completion of the project (accomplishment of district ends). In this way, district ends can be reached in an efficient, systematic fashion, and, most importantly, thereby all stakeholders have some degree of buy-in. As noted by Alsbury and Gore (2015):

> To accomplish these objectives, a district needs an aligned system comprised of three major elements. The first is teaching, which is closest to students and therefore the most critical of the three. Next is instructional leadership from school and other administrators who directly support the classroom teachers. And finally, there is a need for organizational leadership that is aligned with but more operational than instructional leadership. (p. ix)

The key premise of a PLO is that it takes a system to increase student achievement or, as the African proverb says, "It takes a village to raise a child."

HOW THE STRATEGIC TEAM CAN HAMPER THE SUCCESS OF A PLO

When overseeing the organization, the strategic team must always prepare for the unexpected. As Murphy's law states, "Anything that can go wrong, will go wrong."

What problems can arise that will create damage among these three systems? Several problems can arise and must be monitored. Considering our analogy, if the homeowners (strategic/board) are not in agreement about how to build the house (direction of the district), it will lead to chaos and unclear expectations. Unclear expectations often arise when homeowners (strategic/board) fail to work together as a team and seek individual agendas while attempting to direct the contractor (superintendent) regarding priorities.

Although it is acceptable to disagree, it is another matter to allow disagreements to impede decision-making. Sadly, if these disagreements lead to the dismissal of the contractor (superintendent) and subsequent contractors (future superintendents) in this analogy, objectives will not be met in a consistent manner, and staff morale will deteriorate.

Monitoring goals is vital to the success of any project. If the homeowners (strategic/board) fail to properly monitor building plans (goals for the district), it is likely to lead to system breakdowns and a failure to meet home-owner (organizational) goals. Another problem may arise if the homeowners seek to circumvent the contractor (superintendent) and communicate directly with staff regarding how various tasks should be completed.

Micromanagement leads to turnover on all three teams and confusion about roles, duties, and priorities of the purpose of the school district. As noted, of the three systems, the strategic or governance team needs the most to realize its influence over the entire organizational system. Every strategic decision the governance team makes will, in turn, result in multiple opera-tional responsibilities that will impact either positively or negatively the organizational culture.

Chapter Three

A Look at PLC Teams

As previously discussed, PLCs are the subcomponents of the PLO. PLC teams communicate and collaborate with members of their department or team, but they also share information with other PLC teams to enhance synergy within the organization.

As a quick review, PLO is a name used to describe a system of collaboration guided by the governance team and utilized to formulate and carry out district ends by relying on various strategic (governance), tactical (administration), and operational (staff) teams. This requires intentional linkage, especially between the school district and its schools, through the use of mechanisms such as PLCs (Van Clay et al., 2011). Systemic linkage provides the board and other stakeholders with an opportunity to stay abreast of district operations.

PLOs cannot be ultimately effective without strong direction, support, and leadership from the governance team. Therefore, it is vital that the superintendent and the school board (the governance team) share the same philosophy and be in accord regarding the direction of the school district. For this reason, school boards should be meticulous in selecting a superintendent, and I recommend that school boards consult with search firms. Conversely, superintendents should be meticulous as well and not consent to become a district's superintendent for frivolous reasons.

Why is strong leadership important in PLO organizations? Psychologist Robert Evans provided an answer:

> Major change almost never wells up from the bottom. It begins near the top (and if not, it almost never takes hold without strong backing from the top). It typically starts with a key leader and a small core of people who care strongly about a particular solution to a problem. It spreads out from there. As the process unfolds the need for pressure and support requires the assertion of

executive influence. . . . Authentic leaders develop and maintain their capacity
to apply top-down influence. (as cited in DuFour et al., 2008)

Without strong support from the governance team, creative sparks may occasionally glow or flare throughout the organization, but effective, systemic
change cannot occur without influence and support from the governance
team. This includes having the governance team determine the perimeter of
engagement and other expectations of its learning communities (Carbaugh et
al., 2015). Richard DuFour, author and cofounder of Solution Tree, agreed
and stated:

> We must be "tight" on the fundamental purpose of the organization and a few
> big ideas—insisting those within the organization act in ways consistent with
> those concepts and demanding that the district align all of its practices and
> programs with them. . . . We must encourage individual/organizational autono-
> my in the day-to-day operations of the various schools and departments within
> the district. This autonomy is not characterized by random acts of innovation,
> but rather by carefully defined parameters. (as cited in Van Clay et al., 2011)

Parameters are defined by district ends (mission, vision, goals, and values)
that not only direct PLCs but are a part of the intentional linkage between the
school district and its schools. PLOs recognize the importance of providing
direction without stifling staff creativity. This is yet another reason why
PLOs govern using a "collaborative governance" and/or "balanced governance approach" as compared to hands-off or top-down or "my way or the
highway" micromanagement approaches that are ineffective and often lead to
staff resentment.

During the 1980s, educational researchers favored a hands-off approach
from school boards and argued that the governing authority be redistributed
to district schools. Researchers promoted the idea that district schools should
have the autonomy to drive school improvement initiatives based on their
own creativity and knowledge of school operations. Researchers called for
greater building-level decision-making in areas such as instruction, personnel, budget, and policy. This redistribution of power was tokened "site-based
management."

Site-based management, based on bottom-up influence, led to the misalignment of district priorities and failed to transform public schools mean-
ingfully. On the other hand, too much top-down influence is not effective
either. Top-down management often creates a climate of resentment among
district staff members, as well as a failure to obtain staff buy-in regarding
district expectations. Without buy-in, staff may follow district rules and procedures to the letter, but often they will not go the extra mile of practicing the
true intent of those rules and procedures. As rocker Rod Stewart stated:
"Only a fool permits the letter of the law to override the spirit in the heart."

PLOs are based on a balanced governance approach because it fuses aspects of top-down and bottom-up concepts to create a collaborative governance model. Alsbury and Gore (2015) described balance governance as "a school governance approach that supports and promotes 'balance'— discouraging micromanaging on one end of the governance continuum and a disengaged, rubber-stamping board on the other."

In order for PLOs to work efficiently, governance teams must lead by providing direction to PLC teams by establishing and confirming district ends while at the same time allocating resources for PLC teams to meet those district ends. Furthermore, governance teams must ensure that PLC teams are given the opportunity to engage in systemic collaboration and communications in a mutual effort to meet district ends (DuFour & Eaker, 1998).

MEET THE PLC TEAMS

There is no set number of professional learning communities (teams) a district may have; it may be more or fewer depending upon district needs. PLOs are guided by the key belief that all district staff members (e.g., support staff, teachers, administrators, unit office) should have the ability to collaborate and communicate with peers regarding the implementation of district ends. The superintendent, with the exception of the governance learning team, is the chief facilitator of all PLC teams. It is the superintendent's duty to help identify what PLC teams may be necessary to accomplish district ends and to advance board expectations.

Figure 3.1 depicts an example of a PLO based upon seven common PLC teams: governance, administrative, building, teachers, parents, students, and district learning teams.

PLC teams are interconnected by district ends and have the ability to communicate and collaborate with their peers as well as being informed by other learning teams, as will be explained later in the chapter. *When constructing PLC teams, each district must formulate learning teams based on its unique needs and determine each team's purpose and who will guide the learning teams.* Martin and Rains (2018) provided some helpful advice regarding the structure of learning teams:

- Consider using opinion leaders—individuals who are so well respected within the organization that others are more likely to follow their lead.
- Team leaders should understand individuals' strengths and weaknesses. For instance, relationship-oriented people are often more in tune with people needs and frequently ensure that all voices are heard on the learning team. By comparison, task-oriented people may pay more much attention to details and tasks than on team member needs.

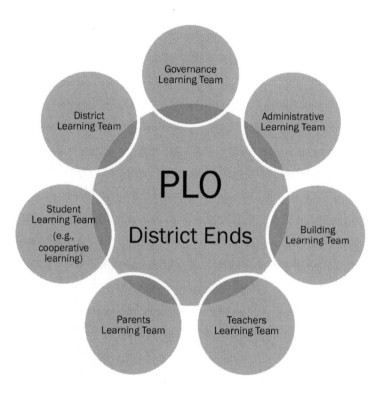

Figure 3.1.   PLC teams

- Keep teams fewer than 10 members; performance problems increase as team size increases.
- Identify individuals on each learning team; being unclear about who is on a team is a common collaboration issue.
- Establish loose–tight leadership. Tight leadership describes mandates that are nonnegotiable such as all students will continuously learn at their own pace. Loose leadership demonstrates flexibility. For instance, staff will ensure increased student achievement and help define how students learn at their own pace.

Below are some general guidelines districts should strongly consider when formulating learning teams, recommended members, and their purpose. Listed below are examples of common PLC teams, suggested members, and each team's purpose.

Governance Learning Team

The governance learning team (GLT) should be composed of school board members and the superintendent. This GLT, headed by the school board, is the most important variable in the PLO for several reasons. The community elects school board members to serve as trustees on their behalf and charges them to clarify and monitor the district's purpose. The school board clarifies the district's purpose by outlining and approving district ends (values and beliefs, mission, vision, and goals).

District ends should be viewed as the district's nonnegotiables and provide the perimeter for which PLC teams operate. Furthermore, it enables systemic alignment throughout the school organization as district personnel work toward common organizational goals in mutually supportive ways. Without systemic alignment, individual school initiatives will compete with organizational goals, because individual school initiatives tend to create their own priorities (Van Clay & Soldwedel, 2009).

Balch and Adamson (2017) noted that the GLT is well positioned to think systemically about school and district improvement when formulating the district's strategic plan because of the focus on the district's core values and beliefs, mission, and vision commitments. Due to this focus, school boards are well positioned to consider a bounded systems approach (a focus on whole or complete systems) when considering school/district strengths and weaknesses. This approach enables members of the board to become "system thinkers," understanding that everything is connected to everything else.

The GLT is also most essential because the elected school board hires the superintendent and charges him or her with the task of carrying out district ends as well as managing the day-to-day operations of the district and providing leadership for the staff. It must be noted that due to the superintendent's job duties, the superintendent is classified as a de facto member of the governance team.

The GLT is also the most essential because it provides the resources that enable PLC teams to thrive. Without support, direction, and resources (e.g., financial) from the governance team, PLC teams will not be able to fulfill their mission. Due to the importance of the governance team, it should set and establish the tone for collaboration, thus serving as an example for how district PLC teams should operate, including following effective group norms as will be discussed later.

The GLT promotes systemic collaboration in a variety of ways, but specifically when developing the district's strategic plan to formulate district ends. Clarifying the district's purpose through formulating district ends is a key responsibility of the governance team; without this direction, PLC teams will become disunited in purpose.

When establishing the district's strategic plan, the governance team practices "collaborative governance" when it solicits internal and external stakeholder input by relying on focus groups, surveys, and/or deliberative polling. This concept can also be described as civic capacity.

Carbaugh et al. (2015) defined civic capacity as

> the ability of business leaders, union leaders, civic leaders, educational leaders, and leaders of other significant organizations to work together on behalf of common goals. Developing such civic capacity builds trust, a common identity, and the willingness to work with shared purpose for the success of the school or schools within the system.

The GLT, in an effort to role-model collaboration and to seek buy-in regarding district ends, allows for various stakeholders to have a voice in the direction of the district when engaging in strategic planning or goal setting as illustrated in Figure 3.2.

The strategic plan is the glue that links the PLO system together based on collective common interests and goals. When stakeholders feel valued and

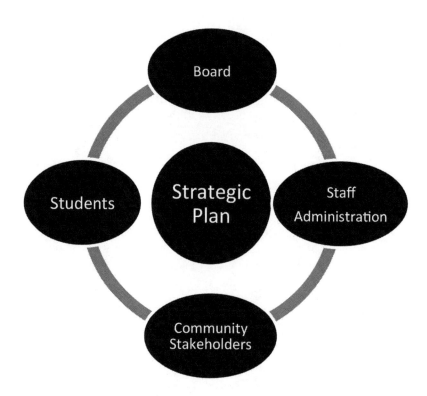

Figure 3.2.   PLC teams providing input and strategic planning

maintain the belief that their voices are heard, stakeholders are inspired to go above and beyond the call of duty to accomplish organizational goals. Although the GLT should welcome stakeholder input, the GLT must strive to ensure that stakeholders understand that although their voices are valued, the GLT will ultimately make any final decisions regarding the direction of the district. Nevertheless, the GLT should genuinely strive to consider and meet the needs of the stakeholders. According to IASB (2018), this concept is often referred to as the "promise to the public."

This "promise to the public" is based on the concept of the board being clear about its rationale for convening the community and the expectations it holds for itself and for the community regarding soliciting community input (IASB, 2018). For instance, the board may promise to listen to all voices in the community, seek to understand community interests, utilize community feedback to advocate for community support regarding those interests, and keep the community properly informed about the use of community input. Also, the board may expect the community to convey what it expects from the governance team, offer honest information, understand that the GLT will make final governance decisions, and support the process for which decisions were made (IASB, 2018).

As noted, in a PLO model the governance team has a duty to monitor student achievement and organizational effectiveness and ensure that all stakeholder voices are heard. Besides the strategic plan, there are a myriad of ways that GLTs can ensure that policies and procedures are in place that allow for stakeholder voices to be heard while ensuring that a district chain of command is followed.

Altamont Community Unit 10 School has adapted an internal document titled "SBAR" (Situation, Background, Assessment, Recommendation) similarly used by the military, aviation, and health care systems that allows employees to initiate and/or advance ideas or other areas of concern (see Figure 3.3). If employees have an idea or concern, they are empowered to complete a SBAR form (see Textbox 3.1) and submit it to their immediate supervisor or person designated. If the supervisor cannot properly solve the problem, it goes to the next person in authority and so forth, with the school board being the final entity. For example, a sample protocol chain may look like Figure 3.3.

Figure 3.3. Chain of command/sample protocol

TEXTBOX 3.1. SITUATION BACKGROUND ASSESSMENT RECOMMENDATION (SBAR) SAMPLE DISTRICT COMMUNICATION

Please utilize the following format to initiate, advance, and review district discussions on issues that span levels of governance: end user–administration–school board.

Topic:_____

S

Situation: Describe current status or issue/concern and/or idea.

B

Background: Provide pertinent information relating to the history of this topic.

A

Assessment: Provide your assessment of the issue/topic.

Include estimates, benchmarking, comparisons, and options you have considered.

R

Recommendation: Please provide your recommendation to address this issue.

Signature of initiator of the form and contact information:

_____

Administrator reviews and dates: _____

_____

Administrator notes/recommendations: _____

_____

_____

Board reviews, actions, and dates: _____

_____

_____

_____

_____

It is vital for the GLT to codify through written policies its expectations for the district. It should also be noted that the first and ultimate duty of the school board in establishing and maintaining a PLO system is to ensure good governance on the governance team. Without good governance and cooperation, the best of reform initiatives will fall by the wayside. In addition, there are several areas the GLT must establish and monitor to successfully lead the PLO system (Cunningham, 2016; Marzano & Waters, 2009).

Overall, the vital leadership responsibilities of the governance team to develop and/or sustain the PLO (from a strategic as compared to an operational role) are as follows:

1. Ensure that governance (school board) and operational (staff) roles and duties are adhered to.

    a. GLT defines the "what" and district staff defines the "how."
    b. The "how" allows for "defined autonomy" to meet goals.
    c. Policies are reflective of district practice.
    d. The board participates in board self-evaluations and governs through the use of process agreements or operational norms.
    e. There is an identified chain of command.
    f. The GLT participates in professional development.
    g. New board members are properly oriented.

2. Guarantee systems of communications and input that encompass all district stakeholders (internal and external) and monitor the level of trust between the district and its schools.

    a. The district requires everyone to communicate and collaborate based on respect for all stakeholders (e.g., see SBAR form above).
    b. Collaborative group norms are identified in district/school learning communities.
    c. Vital information discovered in this collaborative work is shared districtwide.

3. Ensure collaborative governance regarding the establishment of a district strategic plan (formulation of district ends: mission, vision, values, and district goals).

    a. This entails creating board alignment with and supporting district goals.

    b. It includes allocating resources to support the goals for achievement and instruction.

    c. This also means linking district, school, and team goals (staff is pulling in a common direction).

    d. This entails reviewing school/district improvement plans.

4. Establish nonnegotiable goals for student achievement and instruction.
5. Help to clarify and monitor what students are to learn.

    a. Monitor achievement and instruction goals.

6. Establish accountability and/or a focus on results, based on continuous improvement of the curriculum, which is based upon the following:

    a. clarifying what students are to learn (guaranteed curriculum),

    b. assessing student learning (promoting the use of common assessments, being cautious not to be data rich and information poor),

    c. responding to students who are not learning,

    d. responding to students who surpass learning expectations, and

    e. acknowledging and celebrating district success.

7. Ensure systems for capacity building.

    a. Systems are put into place to orient new hires to the district collaborative culture.

    b. Ensure institutional knowledge is sustained despite resignations, retirements, and terminations.

    c. Conduct exit interviews to monitor organizational climate.

    d. Create a plan for succession planning (e.g., new superintendent search).

Administrative Learning Team

The superintendent may form an administrative learning team (ALT) consisting of district office administrators (e.g., assistant superintendent, director of instruction and curriculum, director of special education) and building principals. Duties of this team include determining regulations, developing and/or reviewing operating procedures, helping to manage complex change (vision, skills, incentives, resources, action plan), identifying resources needed regarding day-to-day operations, engaging in district-level problem solving, and formulating an action plan to accomplish district ends (including time frame and personnel needed) and other governance team outcomes.

The action plan or the "how" should address the following governance team expectations that were described above (Cunningham, 2016; Marzano & Waters, 2009).

1. Ensure that governance (school board) and operational (staff) roles and duties are adhered to and that staff are aware of the chain of command.
2. Guarantee systems of communications and input that encompasses all district stakeholders (internal and external) and monitor the level of trust between the district and its schools.

   a. Maintain communication regarding the district's purpose and priorities.
   b. Monitor building level leadership in providing a collaborative culture.
   c. Learning communities govern by operational norms (see below).
   d. Ensure that the district governs through a network of collaborative teams.
   e. Ensure that learning teams are guided by a focus on learning, and on collaborative culture and are results oriented.

3. Ensure collaborative goal setting (formulation of district ends: mission, vision, values, and district goals).

   a. Ensure the creation of a strategic action plan, or the "how," that aligns the work of schools to district ends, or the "what."
   b. Identify and communicate district priority areas.

4. Establish nonnegotiable goals for student achievement and instruction to ensure that measurable goals are in place.
5. Help to clarify and monitor what students are to learn (accountability or a focus on results).

   a. Ensure a guaranteed and viable curriculum (core curriculum).
   b. Guarantee teachers are provided copies of local, state, and national learning standards.
   c. Ensure that staff helped to develop a district curriculum.
   d. Provide necessary resources.

    e. Provide guidance on interpreting data.
    f. Celebrate successes.

6. Ensure systems for capacity building.

    a. Provide professional development that is aligned to district/ school goals.
    b. Have a process in place to ensure quality personnel that aligns with district expectations.
    c. Guarantee an orientation program for new hires.
    d. Have a succession plan.

When the action plan is completed, the superintendent can submit the plan to the school board for final approval. The ALT should discuss additional ways to support staff work (district learning teams) such as:

- Support staff in meeting districtwide goals including how resources will be distributed (e.g., ensuring common staff plan times and professional development opportunities).
- Assist staff in forming conclusions concerning student data (e.g., limitations to the data; what the data doesn't tell us).
- Establish systems in order for staff periodically to measure student academic performance.
- Ensure that student data is easily assessable for staff members and is easy to analyze.
- Ensure student data is used to make informed decisions concerning student progress.
- Monitor the overall work of district learning teams (e.g., ensure outcome-driven agendas, team norms, and SMART (strategic, measurable, attainable, realistic, and time bound) goals developed to improve student performance).

ALTs are of extreme value to building principals and other school administrators, since these team meetings assist school administrators in carrying out district expectations and help them determine that school operations are not misaligned with district expectations. Moreover, school administrators can better communicate with school staff about district expectations.

ADMINISTRATIVE LEARNING TEAM
GUIDANCE ON TEAM NORMS

A major responsibility of the ALT is to ensure that district learning teams create meaningful operating norms or nonnegotiables that must be present on all teams. Norms signify the standards of behavior by which district learning teams agree to abide in order to work more collaboratively. Norms detail how members will communicate and form consensus, and the norms include a promise that team members will be respectful. Besides some key operating norms, the ALT must allow each team to develop its own set of operating norms.

Group norms are valuable to the success of teams. American author Adam Grant once stated, "The culture of a workplace—an organization's values, norms and practices—has a huge impact on our happiness and success." You can have talented individuals on district learning teams, but if they fail to work collaboratively, they cannot accomplish great things for the school district. As Michael Jordan, former U.S. basketball player, noted, "Talent wins games, but teamwork and intelligence win championships."

The lack of collaboration was realized with the 2006 USA basketball team. The team was composed of 12 NBA superstars and had a successful coaching staff. Despite this, the United States finished third in the world games, losing to Greece, a team with not one NBA player. According to Gregory (n.d.), various international newspaper reporters wrote lines such as "Show me a team of misfits playing like 'a team' and they can beat superstars any day." As noted, in order for district teams to succeed, they must have the right operating norms.

Internet corporation Google is known for conducting research. In 2012, Google discovered that group norms (standards of behaviors for company teams) were essential in determining if company teams were successful in their tasks. The firm studied hundreds of its teams to determine why some company teams soared and others did not. Based on this research, team compositions such as people who shared similar hobbies, had similar personalities, and/or were even composed of friends did not determine whether a group would be successful. Regardless of how teams were arranged, they still had different levels of effectiveness (Duhigg, 2016).

As the research continued, Google began looking at group norms or the behavior of different groups. Google eventually determined that understanding and influencing group norms was vital to improving teamwork. In other words, how team members were treated in their groups was a significant factor in determining a group's success. As Duhigg (2016) noted:

> What distinguished "good teams" from the dysfunctional groups was how teammates treated one another. The right norms, in other words, could raise a group's collective intelligence, whereas the wrong norms could hobble a team, even if, individually, all the members were exceptionally bright.

According to Google's research, effective teams must pay attention to *five key behavioral norms*: psychological safety, dependability, structure/clarity, meaning, and impact (Duhigg, 2016).

1. *Psychological safety*: Team members felt safe to take risks and be vulnerable in front of each other; they took risks without fear of ridicule.
2. *Dependability*: Team members finished things on time and met a high standard of excellence.
3. *Structure clarity*: Team members had clear roles, plans, and goals.
4. *Meaning of work*: Work was personally important to team members.
5. *Impact*: Members believed their work mattered and would help lead to meaningful change.

At a minimum, the ALT must make sure that all district teams incorporate the five norms. These norms are vital in maximizing team member collaboration, because team members must pay attention to how all members of the team are treated. Sample team norms may include the following:

• Consider all viewpoints.
• Be on task and be prepared and follow a scheduled agenda.
• Team members understand their roles and expectations as well as follow the lead of team facilitators in order to ensure structure and efficiency.
• Decisions are based on data (meaning).
• Seek feedback from all team members (a team member's work and opinions matter).
• Be supportive of each team member and maintain a positive attitude.

When teams operate with norms, each member of the team understands how to communicate, how shared decisions will be handled, when to arrive for meetings, and how to disagree in a professional and polite manner. The ALT must help district PLCs see themselves in relation to the overall aims of the organization and see that their work matters. Remember, the ALT helps establish the tone in various learning communities.

Teacher Learning Team

When discussing PLCs, teacher learning teams (TLTs) are generally viewed as the flagship of the PLC model because the concept of learning communities first originated with teachers as an alternative to the isolation in which teachers worked. Furthermore, teachers represent the operational role of the educational process that directly influences student learning. Experience and research shows that what teachers know and can do is perhaps the most important indicator regarding student learning.

The term *PLC* is frequently used to describe teacher learning teams. But, as noted, PLCs are more than teachers. There are actually a multiplicity of learning teams that compose the PLO. What are TLTs? As the name suggests, TLTs are composed of teachers who work collaboratively to share resources and to ensure that similar assessments are being utilized.

Often a TLT collaborates by meeting periodically as a department (social studies, English) and/or grade level (second, third, fourth). It is common for TLTs at the junior high and high school levels to be designated by department whereas elementary schools are by grade level. The basis of TLT work is collaboration. Therefore, a key task of a TLT is formulating their operational norms. The TLT's work is guided by the following principles:

- Clarifying what students are to learn (e.g., unpacking learning standards)
- Determining if students are learning
- Responding appropriately when students are not learning
- Enriching the learning for students who are proficient at learning

To ensure student learning, TLTs unpack student learning standards, which requires a great deal of time and effort. Unpacking learning standards entails the above and determines the following: What do the standards mean? What are the learning targets? What would it look like if a student could do this? What level of rigor is associated with the standard (federal, state, or local), and how is this impacting instructional strategies?

TLTs play a vital role in ensuring that every student will have access to a uniform curriculum, common goals, and assurance that all teachers will be learning from each other in their journey to becoming master teachers (DuFour et al., 2008). Students need this type of *equity* to guarantee that they reach their fullest potential and to prepare for satisfying and productive lives.

To monitor student learning and to guide the curriculum, TLTs formulate and/or review various common student assessments to determine if learning has occurred and not simply to add grades to the grade book. For this reason, teacher teams ensure that sound assessments derive from clear, specific, and appropriate agreed-upon achievement targets to gauge student learning. In short, it provides for common goals in the curriculum.

Assessment is the GPS (global positioning system) for instruction. By developing team community expectations for student learning, and by working as a team unit, this work significantly enhances overall student learning and promotes the professional growth of teachers. This approach fosters cooperation and helps to eliminate the competition among teachers, unlike a common side effect of many failed reforms, such as merit pay for individual teachers.

TLTs rely on a series of formative assessments or "assessments for learning" as compared to summative assessments or the "assessment of learning" approach to gauge and promote student learning. What is the difference? Traditionally, teachers used an "assessment of learning" approach, which was infrequent and typically had deadlines to measure achievement (e.g., test to determine if Johnny can divide two-digit numbers). TLTs are based on the "assessment for learning" approach, which are more frequent and which more accurately inform teachers whether students need additional instructional time (assessments for learning are frequent assessments to determine not only if the student can multiply, but add as well).

The traditional instructional approach to teaching is based on the following formula: pretest, teach, and posttest. The "assessment for learning" approach to teaching is based on enhanced formula to teaching, which is: pretest, teach, reteach (if needed), and posttest. TLTs rely on the "assessment for learning" approach because it informs the teacher of where changes need to be made in respect to his or her teaching. The "assessment for learning" approach provides the following benefits:

- Encourages teachers to collaborate to create and align their assessments to monitor student learning
- Provides for common goals in the curriculum
- Informs teachers of where changes need to be made in their teaching
- Allows teachers to share ideas and other methods to improve their teaching skills, such as various intervention strategies
- Provides for various data points to determine the level of student learning

In order for TLTs to be successful, teachers must deliberately choose and desire to work collaboratively with peers. Dr. Theresa Robinson, associate professor and director of secondary education, Elmhurst College, noted:

> The organizational climate and structure of 21st century P–12 schools should be highly collaborative. Collaboration can be a powerful way to meet the academic, social, and emotional needs of students, as well as the professional needs of educators. Friend and Cook (2013) provide a framework for collaboration that has at its core a personal commitment. While schools and districts may mandate collaboration via professional learning communities, teaming, or department meetings, the most essential element is a personal commitment followed by communication skills. Collaboration is a style that professionals choose to use as opposed to an authoritative style, or a more delegating style. I believe a more collaborative approach to planning for instruction and assessment, leadership, and governance has the potential for more powerful, respectful, and goal-oriented interaction between school professionalism. (Dr. T. Robinson, personal communication, June 7, 2018)

By choosing to work collaboratively (personal commitment), teacher teams will not only be more invested in the district's PLO model, but teachers will learn better when working with peers.

Parent Learning Team

In order to enhance the educational progress of students, educators must embrace parent and family engagement programs. Traditionally, educators have viewed themselves as experts rather than equals or partners with parents and family members. As a result, this led to a hierarchical relationship because no thought was given to the family or to the student's perspective regarding educational outcomes.

Educational researchers understand and value effective parental/family engagement programs because these programs impact student academic achievement, behavior in school, self-esteem, career expectations, school attendance, graduation, and socioemotional development (Abulon & Saquilabon, 2016; Bartz, Collins-Ayanlaja, & Rice, 2017).

In a PLO, districts realize the importance of parental/family engagement and expect that each district school will help create, support, and nurture parent learning teams (PLTs). According to Bartz, Collins-Ayanlaja, & Rice (2017), in order to properly support parent learning teams, it is important for educators to do the following:

- Understand the need to work collaboratively with parents/family members
- Understand the need to empower parents/family members and promote shared responsibility
- Interact with parents/family members who are centered on positive relationships and creating an ambience of trust
- Be transparent and share critical information so that parents can help make informed decisions
- Develop a keen interest in the wants, needs, and challenges of parents/family members
- Focus on preventing and resolving conflict between parents/family members and school personnel
- Provide opportunities to help parents/family members become more engaged in the educational process

Student Learning Team (SLT): Collaborative Learning

Today's learners must know how to be knowledge navigators, which means they must be adept at seeking and finding information from multiple sources. Students must know how to evaluate and analyze data and how to work with peers to turn that knowledge into action. Carroll and Doerr (2010) noted that learning is no longer preparation for the job, it *is* the job. In a world in which information expands exponentially, today's students are active participants in an ever-expanding network of learning environments. They must learn to be knowledge navigators, seeking and finding information from multiple sources, evaluating it, making sense of it, and understanding how to collaborate with their peers to turn information into knowledge, and knowledge into action.

Teachers must be active participants in learning environments to meet the needs of today's learner. Teachers must constantly learn from colleagues and from others and then role-model to students how to engage in collective inquiry. SLTs benefit students; teachers can teach students to become knowledge navigators by enabling students to work in groups or engage in "cooperative learning" projects.

Cooperative learning based on active student engagement is an educational approach that entails students working in groups (SLTs) to complete tasks collectively toward academic goals. This learning strategy requires hands-on lessons that allow students to use multiple learning skills and higher-order thinking to construct meaning and knowledge such as cooperative learning and problem-based learning. And, because PLOs are based on the premise of systemic collaboration, cooperative learning allows students to be a part of the process. Research shows more than 900 validations regarding the effectiveness of cooperative learning (Johnson, Johnson, & Stanne, 2000).

Effingham Community Unit School District 40 has invested in a cooperative learning model based on active student engagement titled "Teach to Lead." Teach to Lead is a partnership of the U.S. Department of Education and the Association for Supervision and Curriculum Development. Unit 40 believes that the success of its program is due to the district's belief that teachers must be empowered. The district believes that teacher leadership and input regarding the learning process can significantly foster student achievement (Illinois School Board News Blog, 2018).

The district's model was one of three selected to be shared with other schools as part of a national Teacher Leadership Lab. The program consists of five pillars: control, empower, collaboration, application, and celebration. A key cornerstone for the district is the level of collaboration that occurs with teachers and students. Teachers periodically meet to discuss learning outcomes and objectives, and cooperative learning projects are designed to teach students problem-solving skills, teamwork, technological skills, and real-world applications (Illinois School Board News Blog, 2018).

In short, teachers have a critical role in ensuring that students are "knowledge navigators" by teaching students how to appropriately work with peers. Who is better trained than our teachers? Unit 40 is correct in its belief that teachers are experts in schools and instruction, and as such, should be supported to lead the key changes and innovations that their students, colleagues, and profession deserve to do their best work every day. Cooperation and collaboration instead of competition based on standardized tests must be an area of focus in the 21st century.

Building Learning Team

Building principals should form building learning teams (BLTs) composed of key building staff members to facilitate school operations, support school-wide initiatives, and assist with managing the affairs of the school. Typically, this includes department chairs, grade-level teacher leaders, counselors, and teacher aide leaders. The duties of this team include:

- Coordinating all-staff building meetings to:

  - Clarify the school's purpose and/or mission
  - Develop a school improvement plan (ensure the plan is linked to district ends)
  - Identify collective commitments
  - Create a sense of urgency concerning district/school priorities

- Developing communication procedures

  - Internal/external stakeholder communications (school–community relations, teacher–parent communications, parent groups, and staff protocols for dealing with issues)
  - Informal networking with opinion leaders

- Addressing/discussing building concerns
- Overseeing building TLC/support staff teams (e.g., reviewing meeting agendas and ensuring team operational norms are in place)

  - Ensuring that the collaborative team's mission is clear and concise (focus on learning, collaborative culture, focus on results)
  - Providing appropriate resources to learning teams
  - Providing assistance with how to interpret data

- Developing and/or reviewing building protocols (e.g., safety)
- Planning/implementing schoolwide initiatives and celebrating success
- Assisting in planning a guaranteed and viable curriculum

  - Providing assistance with federal, state, or local student assessments

- Ensuring that teachers are provided copies of various learning standards and assisting in soliciting staff input regarding the district's curriculum guide
- Ensuring that staff knows and understand how to "unpack" learning standards
- Providing resources to struggling learners and those who meet or exceed learning expectations
- Formative and summative assessments are used to guide instructional strategies.

- Assisting with staff professional development needs

  - New teachers are mentored.
  - Staff development is maintained.

The BLT ensures that staff has time to collaborate often by grade level and/or department. Furthermore, the BLT suggests professional development opportunities and assists in providing and distributing resources.

Figures 3.4 and 3.5 illustrate how TLTs share information to the BLT regarding school operations.

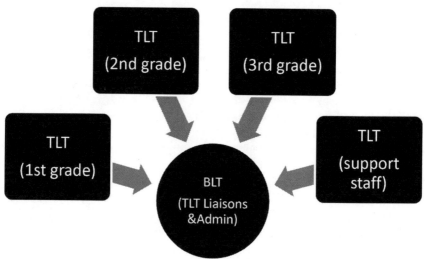

Figure 3.4.   Teacher learning teams providing input to the building learning team

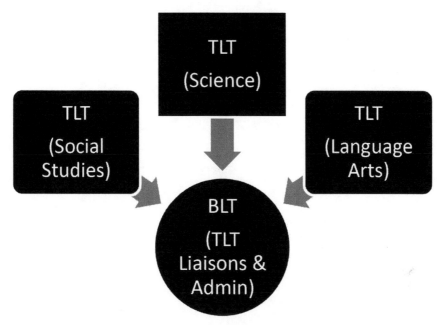

Figure 3.5. Teacher learning teams providing input and building learning team

District Learning Team

The district learning team (DLT) is composed of various stakeholder representatives from each of the district's PLC teams. Representative members may be chosen from the following PLC teams: board of education, administrative team, teachers from various schools, counselors/social workers, and various community groups. The ultimate purpose of the DLT is to serve as a point of information for all PLC teams. It is to provide an equal opportunity to keep all PLC teams apprised of school/district/community resources, as well as an opportunity to review and discuss how PLC teams are meeting organizational goals.

DLT representatives can share information learned with members of their respected schools or areas, which will provide an awareness of what is occurring throughout the district. Sharing information is necessary in order to build relationships throughout the district and to generate the belief that district stakeholders are working collaboratively to meet organizational goals as opposed to operating as individual school units.

Chapter Four

The Power of Informed Oversight and Systemic Governance

School boards often struggle with how to stay properly informed of district operations, often due to uncertainty about when, and how much, information is needed by the board in order to govern effectively. Why is this important? School boards are known by the decisions they make, and they are often criticized for the decisions they have to make in an effort to balance community values of liberty, equality, prosperity, and community (Boyle & Burns, 2011).

If school boards are to govern effectively in the 21st century, they must have access to essential information in order to have a thorough understanding of how the district works to properly forecast future district operations. This includes having an awareness of the day-to-day operations of the district provided by multiple stakeholders without stepping on the toes of the superintendent or engaging in "micromanagement" practices. Nevertheless, access to information places the board in the driver's seat as trustee and enables the board to make sound governing decisions.

School boards must be properly informed of school operations primarily because various laws designate authority to boards to adopt and enforce all necessary policies and procedures for the management and governance of schools under its jurisdiction. The board is the only elected entity charged with the sole responsibility of governing the district. Therefore, it is ultimately the board's responsibility to monitor the effectiveness of the organization in implementing district ends.

The right to obtain information is critical as boards are expected to be prepared when communicating with stakeholders concerning district operations. For instance, when significant problems occur in the district, internal and/or external stakeholders are increasingly looking to the board for answers and demanding accountability regarding a myriad of issues, such as district financial matters, staff morale, and student achievement. Of these issues, school boards increasingly in the last decade have been asked to address student achievement, which is a significant break from tradition.

Traditionally reformers have directed their focus regarding student achievement deficits to classroom teachers to principals, shifting in recent years to superintendents to school boards (Alsbury & Gore, 2015).

Since boards indirectly create the conditions for learning to occur, many reformers are reexamining how the board may positively influence student achievement in other ways and whether they should have and/or have the capability to do so. Moreover, increasingly boards are becoming unsure of their role because community stakeholders are expecting boards to know everything about district operations. Complicating this issue is the fact that 22 states mandate board training in an effort to hold board members accountable for a plethora of things related to district operations and/or school board governance (Rice, 2014).

As volunteers, many board members are blindsided upon taking their seats and are simply not aware of the growing number of expectations they are to encounter, which contributes to role confusion and micromanagement between the school board and superintendent. Professional development is needed to inform boards about their roles and duties, including various complexities of board governance. PLO districts enable the board to govern the district responsibly by relying on a balanced, holistic approach in keeping the board informed while respecting the roles between the board, administration, and other staff members.

It is incumbent upon governance teams to realize that when school boards are misinformed, they cannot properly understand the pulse of the district, which often jeopardizes the board's credibility as a governing entity. The board's credibility is jeopardized when the board is caught off guard by some significant district issue. For example, there are many boards that have been made aware of "a vote of no confidence" concerning the superintendent or another district administrator via staff members, developments to which the board was unaware. As tensions increased, stakeholders looked to the school board for answers to key questions, such as, "What did the board know about the particular issue, when did the board know it, and what actions were taken by the board to address it?"

Because district stakeholders rightfully believe the buck stops with the school board regarding overall district operations, the board must understand district operations not only to govern effectively, but to avoid being "surprised" or blindsided as well.

INFORMED OVERSIGHT

Informed oversight is the name given to school boards, especially those in PLO districts that have a thorough understanding of how the district operates, and to boards that verify the information they receive to ensure its accuracy. Informed oversight is rooted in the concept of "trust but verify," which entails the triangulation of data. Informed oversight enables the board to better understand the means or process and procedures required to reach district ends. Why is it important for the board to be thoroughly informed about district operations? Research informs us that well-informed school boards are more effective in governing than those that are not.

According to the Iowa Association of School Boards' Lighthouse study (2000), characteristics of effective school boards, in contrast to ineffective districts, included the following:

- Being knowledgeable about teaching and learning and how staff collaborated throughout the district
- Having access to data to make data-driven decisions
- Knowing and citing examples of how district policies were being implemented
- Having an overall awareness of district operations (e.g., curriculum, instruction, assessment, staff development, and learning conditions of their schools)
- Understanding the purposes/processes of school/district improvement initiatives
- Identifying specific examples of how board goals were being implemented; staff could link board goals to building goals
- Relying on information from various sources or governing by informed oversight (e.g., reports from the superintendent, curriculum director, principals, and lead teachers) to monitor district ends

In comparison, uninformed boards often are not aware of district operations, and are more likely to engage in micromanagement to make changes or simply govern using a hands-off approach.

As noted, the concept of "trust but verify" is essential to the governing concept of informed oversight. Trust but verify entails how the board can validate information by relying on various verification processes. This level of transparency strengthens the trust between the board and the superintendent and fosters board confidence in its chief administrator. Admittedly, the concept may seem like an interesting paradox, but research consistently supports the notion that effective districts are led by highly informed school boards that utilize various verification processes (e.g., triangulation of data) to ensure that district ends are being met (IASB, 2000).

The concept of "trust but verify" does not entail the board engaging in micromanagement of the superintendent. Rather, it means creating and establishing a PLO system whereby the superintendent is responsible for leading the organization on behalf of the board while simultaneously ensuring that the board has a good vantage point to ascertain how district work is being carried out—in other words, informed oversight. If the board is uninformed about district operations, the board may be prone to asking a myriad of questions related to operations and management and possibly an effort to micromanage.

Alsbury and Gore (2015), in their book titled *Improving School Board Effectiveness*, discussed how informed oversight is the careful management and supervision of the district based upon a thorough understanding of how the organization works. It must be emphasized that informed oversight is not micromanaging the superintendent; it is working collaboratively with the superintendent. Informed oversight entails the board trusting the superintendent but also verifying information as needed.

For instance, when school boards engage in goal setting, it is common for boards to discuss how they will monitor district goals based upon the information the superintendent arranges or provides to demonstrate progress toward district goals. Informed oversight empowers the board to establish and monitor district ends and/or policy centered on student learning and organizational effectiveness. It enables the board to better understand the means or process/procedures that are required to reach district ends (Alsbury & Gore, 2015).

Using a symphony analogy, a PLO is distinctive in that it creates a system whereby the superintendent is the conductor, responsible for directing the performance of staff (those with the expertise to meet organizational objectives), which in our analogy are the musicians. The board is the audience, observing the superintendent/conductor at work, and hearing the unique contributions of various musicians/staff members to discern how these contributions are coalesced to make beautiful music (the meeting of organizational objectives).

In essence, PLOs provide the board with an opportunity to monitor and shape the organization through macromanagement practices, or the act of leading, guiding, and directing the superintendent and other staff members through board policy. This is reflected by Miles Anthony Smith (2012), author and speaker, who coined the phrase "Macromanage not micromanage."

TRIANGULATION OF DATA

PLOs provide boards with a working model of how to effectively obtain information the boards need to govern while using the concept of trust but verify. In order for the board to adequately trust but verify, the board uses triangulation of data or using multiple data sources to produce understanding (Qualitative Research Guidelines Project, n.d.). Why is triangulation of data important? Researchers have long considered triangulation of data to be important to corroborate findings, as well as to test for validity. More importantly, triangulation helps to ensure that information is rich, robust, and comprehensive (Qualitative Research Guidelines Project, n.d.).

In PLO districts, boards triangulate data by relying on and examining a variety of data sources (e.g., PLC teams), including different points in time, and by analyzing various viewpoints of internal/external stakeholders as will be discussed. Triangulation helps the board to understand the data better as it seeks more fully to understand the operations of the district and to ensure systemic collaboration and communication. Furthermore, if triangulation is vital to researchers for testing various theories while advancing knowledge, shouldn't boards also rely on various data sources, as compared to relying on a single individual or data source?

In addition, given the myriad problems school boards encounter as trustees, how could the board effectively deal with issues without access to good data and the ability to communicate with various stakeholders regarding district ends?

In short, a PLO board "trusts but verifies," or triangulates the information it receives regarding district ends and operations by using a holistic approach. This allows for greater transparency, the validation of data, and opportunity for key stakeholders to give voice regarding the direction of the district. Consequently, this enhances the three big ideas of PLO districts (focus on learning, results, and collaboration). It is important to note that the concepts of trust but verify or triangulation of data should not be misconstrued to suggest that a spirit of mistrust exists between the board and its superintendent and/or that the board is simply attempting to second-guess or micromanage the superintendent.

Using a bank analogy, if individuals are receiving cash back from their bank teller, most individuals will recount the money they receive to ensure its accuracy regardless of the relationship they have with the bank. Most banks welcome this accountability to ensure financial accuracy and do not view this action as a form of mistrust. Likewise, governance teams should strive to ensure accuracy and to demonstrate accountability and transparency in their charge to enhance student learning and organizational effectiveness.

Systemic trust throughout the PLO system is a must, especially between the school board and superintendent. Superintendents should welcome transparency without fear and/or reprisal of the board playing "gotcha" regarding areas of district dissatisfaction. It must be noted that if trust does not exist between the board and superintendent, eventually the relationship will perish, regardless if the district is a PLO system or not.

HOW INFORMED OVERSIGHT ASSISTS THE GOVERNANCE TEAM (MONITORING ORGANIZATIONAL EFFECTIVENESS)

PLOs thrive because they foster the entire school district with clarity concerning the establishment and progress toward organizational goals from the boardroom to the classroom. Besides the board being properly informed of district operations, district staff members will better understand the operations of the district as well. What is the key that allows this to occur? Informed oversight entails various reports given to the board from various PLC communities within the district.

The key is a systemic network of learning communities sharing data and working collaboratively. And, with the board at the helm, the board properly ensures organizational effectiveness as various learning communities provide periodic reports to the board.

Traditionally, boards are taught to rely on the superintendent for all the information they desire regarding district operations. This is a key concept of policy governance or the belief that "the board formulates and approves policy while the superintendent implements policy."

PLO districts believe in the key concepts of policy governance, specifically that the school board should work with and through the superintendent to obtain the information it needs to govern. Nevertheless, in PLO districts the board has the expectation that the superintendent will allow other key staff members to provide updates to the board as well, because information could easily be distorted through the layers. This allows the board to be better informed by the triangulation of information, or using multiple data sources to increase understanding regarding district ends.

In actuality, effective superintendents periodically arrange for various district staff members (such as building principals, facilities director, food services director, and central office administrators) to update the board regarding district ends, programs, and services. Nevertheless, PLO districts are more intentional than others about how and when district personnel will be utilized to keep the board informed, and the district as a whole is systematically communicating with all stakeholders.

When monitoring district operations, systems must be in place for the board to effectively monitor its policy and procedures. This is vital because the board governs through its written policies. Additionally, the board governs through the formation of, establishing, and/or modifying of district ends, or the process of strategic planning or goal setting.

During the strategic planning process, the governance team (board and superintendent) must have clarity regarding how district ends will be monitored. Strategic planning or setting district goals and direction is an excellent way for governance teams to promote the concept of informed oversight, since this should entail a discussion concerning particular types of monitoring data the board needs and if any reports from district PLCs are warranted to ensure district ends are being implemented. More importantly, these conversations are crucial to avoid "surprises" during board meetings, such as the board expecting to receive information or reports that were not communicated, or worse, expecting to review management data.

Besides keeping the board informed of matters directly related to district ends, the board should also be informed of miscellaneous information as well: district success stories, school programs and events, and updates on other school-related activities. Whether or not the board is being updated regarding district ends or other school activities, PLCs play an important role in providing updates to the board.

As noted, in order for the board to be properly informed of district operations in a PLO, various learning communities or teams periodically provide reports to the governance team during board meetings. Although there may exist several or more learning communities in the district, the governance team primarily hears reports from the district learning team (DLT), the building learning team (BLT), and the administrative learning team (ALT), as depicted in Figure 4.1.

It is not necessary for the board to hear reports from teacher learning teams (TLTs) because the board only needs information at the "macro" and not the "micro" level. Receiving reports directly from TLTs contributes to role confusion because it may lead to the expectation that the board should give feedback regarding the means or day-to-day operations of the district, as compared to the board's true work of directing the ends or results that the board would like the district to accomplish. Although it is not necessary for the board to receive reports directly from TLTs, the board receives indirect reports through BLT reports, because TLT teachers help compose the BLT.

When monitoring district ends and/or other board policies, the board and the superintendent (e.g., the governance learning team [GLT]) should discuss and form consensus regarding how and when district PLC reports will be fused into the school board's yearly calendar of events. Besides updates on district ends and/or other board policies, district PLCs should update the board on the important miscellaneous information as well (again, the success stories, school events, etc.). Monthly reports from PLCs are also not necessary for the board to stay abreast of district operations.

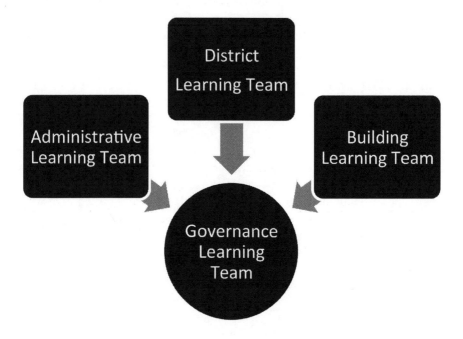

Figure 4.1.   Governance team receiving reports from other learning teams

For instance, BLTs may report quarterly or semiannually, and the ALT may provide quarterly updates. Once an agreement is forged, the superintendent organizes and facilitates the communication between PLCs and the board. The superintendent plays a key role in ensuring that information presented to the board is given at the "macro" level, as opposed to the "micro" level, which would lead to role confusion.

USING ROLE BRIDGERS TO INFORM THE GOVERNANCE TEAM

When receiving reports from PLCs, it is often not necessary for the governance team to hear from a majority of learning team members. A few members of the team, those who serve as role bridgers, can serve as conduits between the various district PLCs and the governance team. Role bridgers are those individuals who can represent multiple PLCs. For instance, the superintendent is a role bridger because he or she can represent both, the strategic (board) and tactical (administration) learning teams. A principal is able to be a role bridger as well, representing the tactical (administration) and operational (staff) role at the respective schools.

Although role bridgers should be utilized to give updates, it is wise to periodically allow for other voices on PLC teams to be heard as well. Superintendent Jean Chrostoski, Goshen County SD #1, described the frequency and content that PLC teams provided to the GLT in stating:

> Our board of education sets aside board meeting time and designates two board-work sessions a year just to look at student data and hear from the curriculum director, principals and teachers on what methodologies they will change and what interventions will be used to assure that all students achieve to high levels. (J. Chrostoski, personal communication, October 3, 2017)

With an active board monitoring district outcomes, Goshen County SD #1 consistently raises student achievement. Receiving reports from key staff members is important as the board needs information to make good decisions. As Shelly Kuhns, board president at Altamont Unit 10, noted:

> As a school board, our role is to make good decisions and provide direction for the district. . . . Although the superintendent works closely with all department leaders to ensure the district goals are addressed, the board needs to maintain open communication with department leaders to ensure systemic collaboration. Despite everyone's best efforts, information is lost or distorted when passed through layers, so it is helpful to communicate directly with the department leaders periodically. (S. Kuhns, personal communication, July 30, 2017)

In order for PLOs to be effective, boards have to monitor district operations effectively and have access to key information from various stakeholders to make informed decisions. If GLTs are neither governing well, nor providing direction, the PLO cannot be sustained. Chrostoski also said:

> No district can be high-achieving unless it has a high-achieving board of education. As superintendent, it is my job to provide [school board members] with the information, professional development and the evidence they need to know that we are providing the best possible learning and educational environment for our students. Only a courageous board can be at the helm, because as the culture begins to change, some staff will leave and new teachers will come on-board which will need mentoring and support to transition into the work our district does. (J. Chrostoski, personal communication, October 3, 2017)

Superintendent Chrostoski's statement is supported by sound research. As Leithwood, Seashore Louis, Anderson, and Wahlstrom (2004) noted: "Effective school and district leadership is crucial for student learning. School and district leadership not only matters, it is second only to teaching among school-related factors in its impact on student learning." The role of the board is key in not only monitoring organizational effectiveness, but also making sure that there is a systemic means of collaboration from the board-room to the classroom.

Chapter Five

Benefits of Becoming a PLO

A district can never become all that it is capable of becoming, or as author Jim Collins (2001) put it, "Go from good to great," without investing in a PLO model. PLOs are second to none in promoting systemic school improvement and equity throughout the organization. DuFour and Eaker's (1998) research reinforces this belief: "The most promising strategy for sustained, substantive school improvement is developing the ability of school personnel to function as professional learning communities."

Educational reformers and politicians have invested in numerous reforms, including charter schools, merit pay, vouchers, and school turnaround models; these changes always lead to modest results, primarily because all too often these market-based school reforms are based on shallow research and have not included input from school boards (Rice, 2014).

Market-based reform efforts are often fragmented and are frequently based on the viewpoints of individuals who are not public K–12 educational practitioners. Further, a market-based business approach leads to the development of a semiprivate public educational system. This must be carefully and skeptically considered, because the primary motivator of any business approach is money, not goodwill.

The PLO approach allows districts to invest in something that works to promote sustained improvement and enables districts to break the cycle of riding the pendulum swing of educational profiteers and the reform organizations that support them. Currently the nation grapples with a teacher shortage due in part to failed educational reforms, bashing of teachers, and raising the requirements for teacher candidates. Reformers mistakenly think the only teacher quality variable that matters is how well an individual scores on a test. There are other variables to consider regarding teacher quality.

The author in the book *Vanishing School Boards* (Rice, 2014) discussed the direct connection of how past educational reforms led to a teacher shortage and the overreliance on alternative certifications. The author noted in Chapters 2 and 3:

> The federal government has pressured states to ratchet up their requirements to ensure that teachers are highly qualified. . . . States such as Illinois have made it difficult for potential teachers to enter the profession by administering rigorous basic skill tests. By shrinking the teaching workforce in public schools, this inevitably impacts local districts because it poses a challenge in recruiting teachers. . . . To become a great teacher, a student needs to know not only content but more importantly how to relate to and reach students. . . . The bottom line is that there are multiple factors that constitute a good teacher. . . . Some states have placed rigorous demands on who can become a teacher, the same does not hold true for most charter school teachers. . . . Is this a plot to manufacture a crisis in education so that the public can support alternatives such as charter schools and alternative certifications? . . . In answering this question, one must wonder why reforms exist that will significantly decrease the number of potential public school teacher candidates. . . . Public school will lack a diverse workforce. Therefore, students of color will be less likely to see teachers who look similar to them. . . . The reformists attempt to sell these reform measures based on the following ideology: unions are the primary cause of low student achievement because they protect novice and inept teachers. . . . "Right-to-work" states have not seen high increases in student achievement compared to unionized states. . . . On the other hand, public school advocates see alternative certifications as a tool to diminish the role of unions and create conditions to further privatize the market. . . . Teacher unions such as the NEA and the AFT survive because they realize that producer competition (e.g., alternative certifications) will hurt unions through contracting out services or organizing nonunion workers, which may or may not be beneficial to consumers. . . . If unions such as the NEA and AFT did not have any say in the hiring and/or dismissal of employees, they will eventually lose membership and perhaps cease to exist. (pp. 31–64)

Unions are already feeling impacts of declining membership. The National Education Association (NEA), the largest teachers' union, has seen a 100,000-person decline in membership since 2010 (Sawchuk, 2014). And, from the 1999–2000 to the 2015–2016 school years, the percentage of public school teachers who participated in a union or employees' association dropped 9% (National Center for Educational Statistics, n.d.).

Regardless of a person's position regarding teacher unions, attacking unions is not the answer to improving our educational system. In fact, states such as Massachusetts and countries such as Finland, which maintain active teacher unions, have been successful in promoting student achievement (Rice, 2014).

When a collaborative relationship exists between management and labor, student achievement and job satisfaction increase. Education attorney Brandon Wright stated, "One of the most important factors in successful bargaining relationships is trust—and trust is almost always connected to the openness and truthfulness of the communication between the parties. Without open and valued avenues for communication, trust tends to disintegrate" (B. Wright, personal communication, October 18, 2017).

PLOs provide for systemic and sustained school improvements, without the need to dismantle the public education infrastructure by investing in reforms that lead to teacher shortages and other unneeded negative disruptions. The secret to the success of PLOs is based on shared collaborative governance.

PLOs can increase the effectiveness of any district. Togneri and Anderson (2003) completed a study on how high-poverty districts beat the odds and increased student achievement. The researchers discovered that districts that believed in the concepts of PLOs improved. These districts believed in collaboration, invested in effective leadership and professional development, built a systemwide framework of instructional supports, and harbored the belief that no stakeholder should tackle reforms alone. All of this led to significant improvements.

PLOs are unique in that they recognize that student achievement requires a systemic collaborative approach from various stakeholders. How can we provide *equity*, and thus ensure that students are successful, if key stakeholders are not consulted? Although the principal and especially the teacher have the most powerful impact on student achievement, there are others stakeholders who play a critical role in establishing the environment so that proper learning can occur (Marzano, 2003). Senge (2006) summed up this concept best when he stated, "What makes an airplane cannot be found in the parts. Likewise for schools: what makes a well-educated student cannot be found in the parts."

Additionally, it must be realized that all teaching is more effective when effectively supported, which requires a supportive and aligned system. Alsbury and Gore (2015) stated that an aligned system is composed of three areas, which PLOs address: teaching (which is closest to students), instructional leadership (the administrators who support teachers), and organizational leadership (which primarily addresses operational concerns).

Faculty, district/school staff, administration, students, community, and parents all have a part to play in ensuring that student learning occurs and, more importantly, these "parts" should be interconnected (Balch & Adamson, 2017). School districts should not be a system of schools, but rather a school system. What is the difference? Van Clay and Soldwedel (2009) stated that a school system is aligned across the organization—vertically, from "top to bottom" across roles, and horizontally in terms of initiatives that don't compete with each other for time and resources. The reverse, a *system of schools*, operates with schools independent of—rather than aligned with—each other and the overall goals of the school organization. A school system is focused and efficient; its staff maximizes time and resources toward meeting the school organization's goals. A system of schools is haphazard and random; although isolated schools may accomplish good things, the overall school organization doesn't change in a focused, continuous way. . . . A challenge for board members is to hold all stakeholders—staff, students, parents, and the other community members in the decision-making process—accountable for the common things that everyone needs to do well. (pp. 5, 25–26)

Collaborative governance and learning teams are not germane to schools alone, since many businesses are investing in the concept of PLCs as well. Best practice for business has moved to collaborative agreement on company ends (mission, vision, and values) and the belief that collaboration provides the best opportunity to maximize company effectiveness (Cunningham, 2016; DuFour & Eaker, 1998).

PLOs are the way of the future because they build human capital. The secret to organizational success is based upon the people who work for the organization. As Senge (2006) noted, "The organizations that will truly excel in the future will be the organizations that discover how to tap people's commitment and capacity to learn at all levels in the organization. It is folly to believe that we can change schools one at a time without the need to invest in human capital."

GOVERNANCE LEARNING TEAM (GLT) BENEFITS

Besides the fact that PLOs are supported by research as an effective way to ensure sustained student achievement based on collaboration, there are several benefits that pertain to why districts should choose to become PLOs. First, we must always remember that leadership starts from the top and that no organization can rise higher than its leadership. Without effective, sustainable leadership, there may be flares of success, but the success will not be systemic. Although districts can identify points of pride, or emphasize what aspects make the district unique, PLOs allow for districts to bind these points of pride together or allow for points of pride to interconnect (Balch & Adamson, 2017).

School boards play a pivotal role in ensuring organizational effectiveness and student learning. It is a mistake for some reformers to bypass local school boards or to view local school boards as part of the problem in boosting student achievement (Cunningham, 2016; Tyack, 1974, 2002).

Educational policy analyst and critic Chester E. Finn referred to school boards as "dinosaurs" and charged that school boards often lag behind in reforms (Cunningham, 2016). Finn continues to be wrong with this outlook and assessment of school boards. Countless school boards are effective and doing amazing work leading their districts. Perhaps Mr. Finn should visit with some of the boards across the country and experience firsthand the hard work and leadership school boards provide for their districts.

Moreover, when the school board and the superintendent govern and lead in their respective roles and take advantage of professional development, it is by far the best school governing model when compared to alternative forms of school governance such as mayoral control (Rice, 2014).

According to Balch and Adamson (2017), a key strength of school boards is the ability to provide systems thinking, but this is often overlooked. According to Van Clay and Soldwedel (2009), systems thinking is grounded in the belief that an institution is complex and often naturally resistant to change, unless change is strategically planned and executed (e.g., strategic plan or district goal setting).

Based on the above premise, it is unlikely that boards could impact organizational change without addressing cultural and structural realities. Thus, PLOs are unique because PLOs solicit stakeholder involvement in decisions that will impact the organizational culture. Because the board provides oversight regarding the day-to-day operations of the district, the school board is well positioned to take a panoramic view to determine how systems interconnect throughout the district.

Superintendent Dr. Nathaniel Cunningham Jr., superintendent of Thornton Township High School District 205, noted:

> Not only is it the job of the school board to provide systems-thinking, but also to direct the superintendent in creating systems to provide meaningful changes. Systems do three things: (1) they find where the failures are, (2) they devise solutions to remediate those failures, and (3) they implement solutions with fidelity. The ability to implement the solution is the key to a quality system. A PLO is unique because it enables the district to support its schools through quality systems. (N. Cunningham, personal communication, July 17, 2018)

Unfortunately, some school boards struggle with how to lead their districts effectively and fail to recognize how systems should work together. Also, some school boards struggle with how to generate effective structural changes that take into account decisions based on community input and other data sources. A key benefit to entice districts to invest in a PLO is that boards will develop the proper understanding of how to drive change appropriately and effectively without the temptation of getting involved in the day-to-day operations of the school district. Furthermore, a PLO model assists the board in fostering trust between the school district and its schools because it relies on stakeholder input and effective communication structures.

A primary function of the school board is to clarify the district's purpose or its reason for existence and to oversee the organizational climate. School boards benefit by becoming PLO organizations because they better understand their role in effectively guiding their districts in fulfilling their purpose. Moreover, PLO districts thoroughly understand the day-to-day operations of the school district. School boards, as well as other PLC groups, have authentic ownership of the success of the district. And school boards can directly see how they influence the day-to-day operations of the district based on the district ends (mission, vision, values, and goals) they have uncovered.

In what additional ways can the school board benefit by becoming a PLO? There are several, including:

- The board will have the ability to make better-informed decisions based on the concept of informed oversight (understand the operations of the district; appropriate access to monitoring data as compared to management data to monitor district success).
- Board governance will be based on collaborative governance and/or a balanced governance approach (balance between being disengaged in district operations and overreaching into administrative areas) (Alsbury, & Gore, 2015).
- Board work will become more meaningful as the board can set and monitor ends more effectively.
- The board can enhance organizational effectiveness and promote equity for students by allowing for shared decision-making.
- The board can take a lead role in establishing a school system as compared to a system of schools.
- The board can enrich community engagement efforts.
- The board will have ability to improve the collective bargaining process by fostering greater trust between management and personnel.
- The board can enhance relationships between board members.
- The board can promote greater transparency and accountability regarding district operations.

ADMINISTRATIVE LEARNING TEAM (ALT) BENEFITS

Administrators benefit tremendously by being a part of a PLO organization. Administrators realize that providing strong leadership encompasses collaborative leadership and does not entail relying on a "top-down" management approach. Sadly, there are many zealous administrators ready to shake up the school system by ushering in what they feel are needed reforms, often without stakeholder support, leading to disastrous results.

Effective administrators realize that they do not have to be the smartest person in the room to become a good leader. Good administrators know the importance of soliciting ideas, investing in people, and building relationships to create change. Thus, PLOs allow administrators to bring about meaningful, sustainable change by being more inclusive. Other benefits include:

- Fostering increased buy-in from stakeholders responsible for carrying out the superintendent's action plan regarding district ends (e.g., mission, vision, goals) and other day-to-day operations of the district
- Experiencing better relationships between the board and the superintendent (helps to ensure that the superintendent is flexible in meeting the needs of the school district, which allows the superintendent to better adapt to changes on the governance team)
- Enhancing the relationships between the superintendent and other district administrators (increased collaboration)
- Enabling the superintendent to become a greater instructional leader by harnessing the knowledge and skills of district administrators

BUILDING LEARNING TEAM (BLT) BENEFITS

It is clear that activities at the school building are the most visible in establishing how the district promotes student achievement. It is at the school building where one can see firsthand the daily instruction being provided to students by teachers, other professionals, and building principals who provide instructional leadership while performing various management duties. To borrow a military phrase, schools are where we see the "boots on the ground" in district operations.

Because school personnel are the most visible in the task of educating students, since the 1980s many educational researchers have favored a "hands-off" approach from school boards and have argued that the governing authority should be redistributed to district schools, which were referred to as "site-based management."

Site-based management led to the misalignment of district priorities and a lack of organizational synergy. Although there are many critics of site-based management, primarily due to this issue, supporters of site-based management deserve credit in their belief that schools should have a voice in the direction of the district and their schools and autonomy in how individual schools carry out district ends. Without sharing a sense of ownership and allowing school staff to be flexible in carrying out district ends, school leaders will stifle staff creativity.

The greatest benefit a PLO provides to the building learning team is that PLOs allow for autonomy but limited autonomy. PLOs allow for some site-based management in how individual schools should be governed but do so in a spirit of collaboration and in harmony with district objectives. In short, this is a balanced governance approach, poised between relying too heavily on either a top-down or bottom-up approach. The building learning team is the entity that provides leadership and arranges collaborative systems at the school level so that school staff can have a voice in the operation of the school and/or district. Other benefits include:

- Improving the relationship between building administrators and school staff
- Establishing systems of protocols for the operations of the school
- Increasing synergy as schools see how they are connected to the overall district
- Fostering creativity and innovation at the school level in meeting district/ school goals
- Enhancing school accountability in meeting district/school goals

TEACHER LEARNING TEAM (TLT) BENEFITS

The teacher learning team (TLT) is very important, especially considering that the concept of PLO/PLC originated from this group's genesis. As previously discussed, PLCs originated from teachers who desired to work more closely with peers after traditionally working in isolation. Unfortunately, most teachers still work in isolation. According to research conducted by the National Council on Teacher Quality (2017) of 100 large school districts, it was discovered that teachers get an average of 45–60 minutes of planning time a day, and seldom if ever is time set aside to work collaboratively with other teachers.

As noted earlier, according to the *MetLife Survey of the American Teacher* (MetLife, 2009), today's teachers still work alone and spend an average of 93% of their time in school working in isolation from their colleagues. As a result, teachers' day-to-day work is disconnected from their peers and their professional development is misaligned with their students' learning needs. Limited resources, poor planning, and lack of administrative leadership continue to prevent teachers from collaborating, as do frivolous reforms such as merit pay, which fosters competition rather than collaboration.

A primary reason to invest in TLTs stems from the fact that teachers remain the professionals who are closest to students to promote learning. For this reason, and as our educational predecessors have determined, the major benefit of teacher learning teams is the ability they give teachers to work with peers to enhance educational opportunities for all students.

Superintendent Chrostoski stated the following concerning the importance of teacher collaboration: "Teacher collaboration has a powerful impact on student performance because instead of having one teacher trying to determine the needs of a struggling student, you have a team of teachers with a variety of expertise working to intervene on behalf of a child" (J. Chrostoski, personal communication, October 3, 2017).

According to research conducted by the New Teacher Center's Teaching, Empowering, Leading and Learning Survey, students who attend schools where teachers are involved in the school and/or district's decision-making processes perform better academically in school. A key finding of the study was that high-poverty districts reported lower levels of teacher involvement (Will, 2017a).

The study further proves that teachers are the ones closest to students and should be given a voice in the direction of the district and/or school. Richard Ingersoll, a professor of education and sociology at the University of Pennsylvania Graduate School of Education, analyzed survey data from approximately 1 million teachers from more than 25,000 schools in 16 states from 2011 to 2015. This was the first large-scale study that measured the impact of teacher leadership on student performance (Will, 2017a).

Unequivocally, student achievement and job satisfaction increase for teachers who work in professional learning communities. Research led by Neena Banerjee, an assistant professor of public administration at Valdosta State University in Georgia, and published in the *American Journal of Education*, studied national federal student achievement data for 5,850 students and their teachers. The researchers discovered that students of teachers who took part in professional learning communities scored better in core subjects such as math (Will, 2017b).

A major benefit of teacher learning teams is helping to close the achievement gap as well as lessen school suspension and other discipline problems with students, especially minority students. Why is this important? Minority and low-income students are more likely to be suspended, more likely to fail classes, and less likely to attend four-year universities as compared to nonminorities (Gewertz, 2017). Teacher learning teams provide an opportunity for teachers to share resources and to hold high expectations for all students.

It is worth noting that teachers from countries, such as Japan, that score well on international tests spend a great deal of time planning, coplanning, conferencing with colleagues, and engaging in other kinds of professional development based on collaboration (Carbaugh et al., 2015). Other benefits related to the teacher learning team (TLT) include:

- They enable teachers to better adapt to ever-changing expectations as educational reforms have too often left educators playing catch-up.
- They promote the sharing of resources among teachers.
- TLTs assist teachers in being more prepared to teach and align curricula and assessments among grade levels.
- They minimize the attempt by parents/guardians to "cherry-pick" teachers, which creates tension (all teachers will teach a common curriculum and share resources).
- TLTs are a tool to orient new teachers and provide the support that beginning teachers need to be successful.
- They assist teachers in better understanding cultural diversity as they work with peers. (Note: According to Maxwell [2014], in 2014 it was projected that for the first time the majority of public school students in that year would be students of color; those making educational decisions are overwhelmingly nonminority.)

TEACHER LEARNING TEAM AND BENEFITS FOR MILLENNIAL TEACHERS

A system of collaboration of individuals from different eras (e.g., baby boomers, years 1946–1964; Generation X, years 1965–1980; and millennials or Generation Y, years 1981–1999) will enhance student learning because differences in values and beliefs exist within all three groups. For instance, baby boomers often prefer competition, are goal driven, are resourceful, value face-to-face communication, value rules and procedures, and are loyal to the organization. Generation Xers are highly independent, are goal oriented, thrive in hierarchical environments, view those in authority as experts, value flexibility, and are linear in their thinking. Millennials, on the other hand, are often dependent on technology, are apt to speak up, and believe their opinions will be heard and valued (Bartz, Thompson, & Rice, 2017).

Millennials expect their work to be judged based on merit, do not like tradition or "that is how we do things," desire frequent feedback, like to work in teams, are more apt to change jobs, exhibit confidence in their work, and love challenges (Bartz, Thompson, & Rice, 2017). Effective administrators harness the power of human capital by taking into consideration the myriad of needs, wants, and different perspectives of various generations.

Presently, millennial teachers generally are supervised by baby boomers and Generation X administrators and are slowly dominating the teaching workforce due to the retirement of baby boomer teachers (Bartz, Thompson, & Rice, 2017). Why is collaboration so important for millennial teachers? Millennial teachers are quick to change jobs if they are dissatisfied with work as compared to previous generations.

Due to unprecedented national teaching shortages, it is imperative that administrators improve working conditions that aid in job satisfaction. To foster job security and reduce turnover, administrators must allow millennials the opportunity to collaborate with peers, express their opinions, give suggestions, ask questions, provide opportunities to be involved in various school/district projects, and be given constructive feedback and coaching.

PLO organizations not only provide various opportunities to foster job satisfaction for millennials, but for all teachers. The bottom line is that if administrators fail to improve working conditions for teachers, not only will we continue to experience a national teaching crisis, but inevitably it will also negatively impact student achievement.

PARENT LEARNING TEAM (PLT) BENEFITS

The primary purpose of the PLT is to partner with school personnel for the sake of positively impacting student achievement, student behavior, self-esteem, career expectations, school attendance, graduation, and socioemotional development. Further, PLTs provide additional opportunities for parents and family members to be more active in the educational process in a myriad of ways, such as serving as conduits regarding community resources, being school volunteers, providing insights regarding school initiatives, and helping to measure school success.

STUDENT LEARNING TEAM (SLT) BENEFITS
(COOPERATIVE LEARNING)

Collaboration should not encompass only adults but students as well. Students should periodically engage in classroom learning teams or "cooperative learning" to enhance pupil learning. Students today are too often given the message that education simply should revolve around them and their own learning needs. How have we created this atmosphere? There is an overemphasis on student testing for honors classes, college admissions, and student rankings in peer groups. Additionally, much attention has been given to students' personalized learning needs, vouchers, and homeschooling that solely centers on the individual learner. Admittedly, we should focus on individual student learning needs, but we must equally teach students the concepts of collaboration and cooperation.

Students, similar to adults, are not islands unto themselves. It is our job as adults to model collaboration for students. As James Baldwin, American novelist and social critic, noted, "Children have never been very good at listening to their elders, but they have never failed to imitate them." When students collaborate, it enhances their learning by illuminating the perspective of others in their quest for knowledge, as we all should be lifelong learners.

As noted earlier, Carroll and Doerr (2010) stated:

> Learning is no longer preparation for the job, it is the job. In a world in which information expands exponentially, today's students are active participants in an ever-expanding network of learning environments. They must learn to be knowledge navigators, seeking and finding information from multiple sources, evaluating it, making sense of it, and understanding how to collaborate with their peers to turn information into knowledge, and knowledge into action. What does this mean for teachers? It means that they should be constantly learning with and from accomplished colleagues and experts in the field, modeling for their students the collaborative learning and knowledge construction that is at the core of 21st-century competencies.

In order for students to be successful, they must learn how to work with others, especially peers. Sparks (2017) noted that

> collaboration is just like any other skill; it has to be taught. The ability to collaborate with others has become of the most sought-after skills in both education and the workplace. A survey by the Association of American Colleges and Universities found that more than 80 percent of midsize or larger employers look for collaboration skills in new hires—but fewer than 40 percent of them considered new graduates prepared to work in teams.

Various student assessments, such as the Program for International Student Assessment (PISA), are beginning to measure the ability of students to have a shared understanding of problems as well as how to solve problems collectively. And, the 21st Century Learning nonprofit organization along with Pearson noted three areas of collaboration that students must know: communicating with others, resolving conflicts, and managing tasks (Sparks, 2017). Educators must teach students how to work more collectively as compared to an overemphasis on competition that leads to selfish ambitions.

Although teachers must constantly learn from colleagues and role-model to students how to engage in collective inquiry, according to the *MetLife Survey of the American Teacher* (MetLife, 2009), teachers spend the bulk of their time working in isolation. In designing PLO systems, again, it cannot be overstated that teachers need time to cooperate with peers, and administrators must be mindful of this when designing teacher schedules.

Based on a review of research by Marzano, Pickering, and Pollock (2001), there are five positive elements associated with cooperative learning:

- Positive interdependence (sense of teamwork)
- Face-to-face promotive interaction (helping each other learn)

- Individual and group accountability (each individual contributing to group goals)
- Interpersonal and small-group skills (communication, trust, leadership, decision-making, and conflict resolution)
- Group processing (focus on team performance)

The researchers also concluded that when students compete with each other, it negatively affects student learning, in contrast to the positive correlations associated with cooperative learning. In what additional ways can student learning teams play a role in the PLO system? The governance team should seek input from students when establishing district goals and direction and/or district ends. Too often we fail to solicit student input in the direction of the school and/or district. For instance, when formulating district ends, the governance team may charge administrators with the task of forming a sort of ad hoc student representative focus group to better understand student concerns.

Further, administrators may consider forming a student council group to discuss various school goals. The bottom line is that a system of collaboration should be systemic throughout the district, encompassing all stakeholders.

DISTRICT LEARNING TEAM (DLT) BENEFITS

A key function of this learning team is the ability to coalesce representatives from the district's learning teams (e.g., governance, administrative, building) and allow for the exchange of information, key updates, and ideas to be learned and shared. Essentially a key strength of this learning team is that it provides for points of information to be shared that are occurring on the district's learning team, as well as any information that should be brought back to the various learning teams. The DLT allows for all stakeholders to stay in the loop regarding overall district operations. Other benefits the DLT provides include:

- Organizational changes that are accepted and embraced
- A forum for the "parts" (e.g., school board, teachers, administrators) of the school system to communicate
- Enhanced awareness of district and community resources
- A sounding board for possible new initiatives
- Enhanced organizational synergy and collaboration

Chapter Six

The Role of the Community Engagement Process in a PLO

This chapter is based in part on the work of Dr. David Bartz, professor emeritus, Eastern Illinois University (EIU), Dr. Cliff Karnes, chairman of the Department of Educational Leadership also at EIU, and Dr. Patrick Rice, director of field services for the Illinois Association of School Boards (2018). The researchers composed an article that appeared in the *National Forum of Educational Administration and Supervision Journal, 36*(4), 1–7, and the Illinois Association of School Administrators journal, *Leadership Matters*, 18–19.

> No form of democratic government permissible under our social contracts is likely to serve an apathetic people well over an extended period of time. Any of the myriad forms for managing schools can function reasonably well so long as substantial numbers of interested and responsible citizens are willing to inform themselves and engage in the task of making them work. (James, 1982, p. 17)

The community engagement process is a key element of a school board's collaborative governance approach and a crucial part of a professional learning community. Each of the school district's stakeholders has a vested interest and a responsibility for creating an environment that maximizes learning for all students in a safe environment through services delivered based on equity. School board members have a tremendous amount of knowledge and support to be gained through the effective use of the community engagement process that complements the professional learning community approach.

School boards are composed of elected officials who are on the front line of a local governmental unit that services the citizens of our great nation. Of the three systems of government—federal, state, and local—school districts, through the collaborative leadership approach of local government by school boards, are the most responsive governmental unit in pursuing and receiving consistent citizen input. Such input is fundamental to a culture that is truly a professional learning organization. Citizens in our nation consistently witness the inability of federal and state governmental agencies to work efficiently, to seek meaningful input, and to be accountable to citizens.

Through the leadership of school boards, school districts are a "shining light" of how a governmental unit should be performing in the democratic process in our country.

Participation in activities, discussions, and decisions that are important to citizens' interests concerning local governmental units such as school districts are perceived as inalienable rights in our democratic society. Social and psychological research has demonstrated that such participation is necessary for the optimal functioning of local school districts. Citizens who perceive they have meaningful input into the school board's decision-making activities that affect their lives—and those of the community's children—through the community engagement process are more likely to actively and fully participate in support of a school district's goals and efforts.

This perceived community ownership is crucial for community stakeholders to fully participate in that process. Such participation creates a sense of responsibility by local citizens for helping to effectuate the school district's goals and to maximize learning for each student through an equitable delivery system (Maehr, Hartman, & Bartz, 1984). The basic principle of the community engagement process is summarized as follows:

1. *Participation*: opportunities through input to the board's decision-making process to establish goals
2. *Commitment* to the board's decisions and goals
3. *Supportive behavior* to accomplish the board's goals (Maehr et al., 1984)

CONTEXT OF COMMUNITY ENGAGEMENT PROCESS

Effective school board members know and understand the importance of keeping "the public" in public schools by engaging in two-way conversations with the citizenry. As elected trustees of the community, board members should establish systems of two-way conversations to ensure local community representation in school governance. These systems enable the board members to actively engage stakeholders in dialogue and in other discourse about the district's vision, mission, and other common interests regarding the schools to improve overall district performance and school climate, while advancing student achievement in a safe environment.

Periodically exchanging information and ideas between various stakeholders and the school board is a primary work of board members and is often referred to as community, public, or civic engagement. Community engagement is a step beyond public relations (PR) because in PR the focus is establishing or maintaining a favorable public image.

Board members with the best intentions sometimes confuse public relations with community engagement. Such confusion results in board members communicating with stakeholders in a one-way fashion that primarily entails sharing positive district news. Public relations efforts are important and should be a part of a community engagement plan, but systems must be in place to allow for two-way communication exchanges. Without these exchanges, stakeholders are limited in their contributions and are likely to feel as though they have no real ownership in the direction of their schools.

Board members should be strategic and thoughtful in developing a community engagement plan. Attempting to engage the public in a haphazard or ad hoc manner will be unsuccessful. The plan should begin with board members having a clear understanding of why they are engaging the community and how this process will result in citizen support for the school district's vision, mission, and goals. Board members need to understand how they can use the results of the community engagement process to contribute to the success of the district. Community engagement needs assessments may be instrumental in assisting boards in their efforts to create a community engagement plan (e.g., see sample needs assessment in Figure 6.1 at the end of the chapter).

A community engagement plan should detail the appropriate level at which the board members desire to engage community members. Board members should initially determine whether they are seeking to inform, consult, involve, or collaborate with stakeholders. Often community involvement gradually increases through these four stages, from informing to collaborating. Board members are encouraged to strive for collaboration, which will, by its very nature, cause them to consult and inform stakeholders. They need to keep the stakeholders continuously informed throughout the community engagement process and after its completion regarding stakeholders' inputs were used and decisions made that flowed from the use of that process.

SUPERINTENDENT/ADMINISTRATION BENEFITS

A good community engagement plan not only benefits the board members, it also provides several advantages for the superintendent, especially regarding board–superintendent relations. As supported by the "dissatisfaction theory" of school governance, when community members become displeased with the board members, that displeasure impacts the relationship with the superintendent, often resulting in turnover. This frequently occurs because the superintendent is viewed as the face of the district.

When stakeholders are satisfied with the governance work of the board members, it increases their longevity as well as the tenure of the superintendent. When longevity of board members is increased, they are in optimal positions to properly establish, monitor, and sustain the district's vision, mission, and goals.

As the superintendent is evaluated, in part, based on implementing district goals and fulfilling its vision and mission, stakeholder satisfaction provides the superintendent with a healthy opportunity to truly establish a professional learning community culture. This is accomplished by aligning board goals established through the community engagement process and supported by the community's stakeholders, with the factors needed to nurture an environment for a true culture reflective of a professional learning community.

A superintendent who consistently engages the public is in a better position to understand the issues of stakeholders and to be proactive in solving future problems. By understanding community issues, the superintendent can proactively inform the board of them, and therefore minimize the chances of board members being surprised or caught off guard regarding potential community reactions.

SPECIFICS OF THE COMMUNITY ENGAGEMENT PROCESS

The community engagement process stresses obtaining input from a diverse representation of stakeholders on key issues related to district personnel delivering the highest possible quality education to each child. A goal of the community engagement process is to forge a partnership between the citizenry and school district. Use of the community engagement process represents an attempt to create joint ownership of goals that include input from community members and a sense of responsibility for accomplishing such goals. The desired outcome of that process is to create a sense of oneness between the local public schools and community members.

At the outset of the community engagement process, the board must make it clear that it is the governing body for the district and the entity that approves and makes decisions. It is equally important that citizens understand the role of their input to the board and administrators regarding perceptions of what needs to be done to maximize learning for each child in the community.

The community engagement process is not a one-shot activity to solicit community input, but rather an extremely well-planned and ongoing pursuit through a number of avenues for collecting citizenry input. This includes sources such as social media, focus groups, surveys, public hearings or input sessions, meeting with various community groups, and even providing a venue for the citizens to provide input to board members and administrators on a one-to-one basis. It is extremely important that board members and administrators involved in the community engagement process understand that the focal point is *gaining input* from stakeholders rather than defending what school personnel are doing (or have done) or by holding debates with stakeholders who have different opinions concerning those actions.

Often a survey instrument is constructed and used as a starting point to solicit input for the community involvement process. It should be noted that a survey is a starting point—not an ending point. Surveys can be conducted online, via telephone, at parent–teacher conferences, or through the U.S. mail. Although online surveys are very popular, there are limitations. For instance, survey results can be skewed in favor of only those responding; therefore, the results cannot be inferred by all the district's citizens. Up-to-date research techniques for telephone surveys (including cell phones) give a better sample, which leads to more confidence that the results are indicative of the beliefs of the total citizenry. This informational data is crucial for helping to gain a snapshot of the community as a whole.

A particular application of the community engagement process is often integrated into a district's strategic planning process. Engaging community stakeholders in strategic planning is a logical and natural process and should result in support for the implementation of the strategic plan's action steps. An initial step in strategic planning is the SWOT (strengths, weaknesses, opportunities, and threats) analysis of the present situation regarding the district's efforts and accomplishments. A SWOT analysis helps identify where the board stands and where it sees itself going in the future. This is an example of a critical time during which the community engagement process can be used for citizens' input (Clark, 2017).

To obtain a broad array of citizen input from a variety of groups, board members must be willing to go out and engage in dialogue with citizens at their locations or on their turf. This communication is critical to the success of any organization. This may require board members and district personnel to get outside of their comfort zones. While not all-inclusive, the information obtained from this engagement should constitute a good starting point for developing or reviewing a district's community engagement process.

Kracke (2006) strongly believes in board members and administrators going out into the community to solicit input where people: (a) worship, (b) study, (c) socialize, (d) work, (e) talk politics, and (f) participate in community service. She also encourages the board to reach out to community leaders to help solicit citizens to participate in the community engagement process. Reaching out to citizen groups at their locations will be a good experience for board members and administrators and should broaden their understanding and context of citizens' input.

KEY ELEMENTS OF AN EFFECTIVE
COMMUNITY ENGAGEMENT PROCESS

While not all-inclusive, the following list represents useful criteria for board members to utilize in planning and evaluating the community engagement process:

1. The purpose is clearly stated and broadly made known to citizens throughout the district.
2. The focus is on understanding the community's aspirations for the education of children in the district.
3. The activities are authentic and respectful of individual citizens and groups providing input.
4. It reflects a high priority and sincere time commitment by board members.
5. It uses social media and other forms of technology to solicit input from the citizenry.
6. It strives to create an oneness and sense of ownership on the part of both board members and the citizenry.
7. It strives to create positive and ongoing relationships between the board members and citizens.
8. The voices of students are sought for input.
9. The board's vision, mission, and policies are inclusive in the process.
10. School board members and their representatives are well trained.
11. The media are used properly to maximize the effectiveness of the community engagement process.
12. Board members must be excellent listeners to all voices in the community, not just to the most vocal and well known.
13. Board members and their representatives physically go out into the community to seek face-to-face input.
14. It communicates the importance of local control of schools and the board's commitment and actions to such control.
15. The board is truly committed to using the input in its decision-making process for the betterment of the district's children.
16. The results are effectively used by the board members for guidance in decision-making.

17. Information is disseminated to the public and to the media regarding how the board used the community's input.

School districts in the United States are at the front line of local control. In most situations, they are governed by board members elected by local citizens. Local control works best when a school district's citizenry has a sincere interest in the schools, provides meaningful input, and is motivated to help make schools the best they can be. The community engagement process provides a venue for meaningful citizenry input to the board members for consideration in their decision-making deliberations and is an essential element in developing a professional learning community. Community engagement also creates a sense of oneness between the board members and the citizenry.

The bottom line is that the effective implementation of the community engagement process will improve education for the community's children.

Community Engagement
(Needs Assessment)

Directions: Please rate your district by circling your response. If an item does not apply, do not respond to it.

Rating Scale:

Strongly Disagree	Disagree	Undecided	Agree	Strongly Agree
(1)	(2)	(3)	(4)	(5)

Items	Your Rating
1. The purpose of the community engagement process is clearly stated and broadly made known to citizens throughout the district.	1 2 3 4 5
2. The community engagement process reflects board members listening to all voices in the community, not just the most vocal and well known.	1 2 3 4 5
3. Community engagement activities stress the board's desire to understand the community's aspirations for the education of the children in the district.	1 2 3 4 5
4. The activities for community members and groups to have input through the community engagement process respect their time availability and are conducted in an efficient manner.	1 2 3 4 5
5. The results flowing from the input received through the community engagement process are effectively used by the board for guidance in its decision making.	1 2 3 4 5
6. The community engagement process activities are authentic and respectful of the individual citizens and groups providing input.	1 2 3 4 5
7. The community engagement process includes a sufficient number of activities for which the board and its representatives physically "go out" into the community to seek input, and not just figuratively reach out for input.	1 2 3 4 5
8. The community engagement process reflects a high priority and sincere time commitment by board members and their representatives.	1 2 3 4 5
9. The community engagement process reflects board members and their representatives as being excellent listeners.	1 2 3 4 5
10. The board uses information gleaned from the community engagement process for the betterment of the children's education.	1 2 3 4 5
11. Proper resources are allocated to the community engagement process in order for it to be successful.	1 2 3 4 5
12. The community engagement process is ongoing.	1 2 3 4 5

Figure 6.1.   Community engagement needs assessment

13. Information is disseminated to the public and media regarding how the board uses the input collected through the community engagement process.	1 2 3 4 5
14. The community engagement process reaches out to all district citizens and groups and is not limited to those with whom board members are likely to agree.	1 2 3 4 5
15. The community engagement process utilizes effective face-to-face interactions for receiving input.	1 2 3 4 5
16. The community engagement process effectively utilizes social media and other forms of technology to solicit input from the citizenry.	1 2 3 4 5
17. The community engagement process is fair and equitable regarding reaching out and considering input from special interest groups.	1 2 3 4 5
18. The community engagement process strives to create a "oneness" and sense of ownership on the part of the board and citizens.	1 2 3 4 5
19. School board members and their representatives involved in the community engagement process perform effectively.	1 2 3 4 5
20. The community engagement process creates positive and ongoing relationships between the board and citizens.	1 2 3 4 5
21. The voices of students are sought out for input through the community engagement process.	1 2 3 4 5
22. The board is truly committed to the concept of a "promise to the public" to use the input in its decision-making process for the betterment of the district's children.	1 2 3 4 5
23. The board's mission, vision, and policies are inclusive of the community engagement process and the "promise to the public" concept.	1 2 3 4 5
24. The community engagement process effectively communicates the importance of local control of schools and the board's commitment and actions to it.	1 2 3 4 5
25. Input sought by the community engagement process through "in person" face-to-face interactions creates an open, inviting, and friendly atmosphere.	1 2 3 4 5
26. School board members and their representatives involved in the community engagement process are well trained.	1 2 3 4 5
27. Individual citizens and groups provide input in a constructive manner.	1 2 3 4 5
28. The board and its representatives work with the media to maximize the effectiveness of the community engagement process.	1 2 3 4 5
29. The board has established procedures for considering input from the community engagement process and uses them effectively.	1 2 3 4 5
30. Overall, the community engagement process has been successful.	1 2 3 4 5

By: David Bartz, Eastern Illinois University   Patrick Rice, IL Assoc. of School Boards

Figure 6.1 *(continued)*

Chapter Seven

Implementation Stages of Becoming a PLO

How to Sustain the PLO Culture

The first step in becoming a PLO is that the district must view itself as a school system and not as a collection of schools. Traditionally we have overly invested in the autonomy of schools (e.g., site-based schools), which has led to many fragmented school systems. Because the burden was too often placed on schools alone to improve academically, effective school administrators (building principals) throughout the country at various times and degrees have invested time and energy in an effort to ensure that a high level of collaboration exists among staff and between staff and other internal (e.g., district personnel) and external stakeholders (e.g., parents and community members) in order for their schools to improve academically.

It is plausible that many school administrators practiced the values and various tenets of structured PLO models without defining them as such and/or relied on various resources to aid them in establishing and sustaining a collaborative PLO (commonly referred to as PLC) culture. In addition, commonsense thinking suggests that not all administrators had the same level of support from internal district stakeholders (e.g., superintendent, central office staff, and/or the school board).

If administrators do not have the support of those highest in authority to patronize a collaborative system, it is unlikely that a collaborative culture could exist, as PLOs must be systemic and supported districtwide to be ultimately successful. Therefore, the GLT or those highest in authority (as opposed to only school building administrators) must also realize the value of PLOs and spearhead the effort to ensure that PLOs are systemic and supported districtwide.

Due to a number of variables, school districts are at different places on the spectrum regarding their PLO implementation. For instance, there are districts that the governance and/or administrative team are leading the charge to ensure PLOs are implemented with fidelity. Similarly, there are individual schools in districts that are attempting to become unilateral PLOs with various degrees of support from the central office. Finally, there are other school districts that have yet to begin any formal or informal process to become PLOs.

Districts may choose not to identify themselves as PLOs because they are missing resources to develop and/or sustain a robust PLO, although they agree with PLO tenets. As a result, some school districts have minimized their views regarding the importance of collaboration and/or stopped supporting preexisting collaborative systems. This is generally because their existing systems did not align with the expectations of what composes a PLO among various members of the world of academia. As a result, some districts may have gradually stopped investing in becoming a PLO when they deemed the work too tedious or time consuming.

Districts must remember that becoming a PLO is a process and not an event. Districts should not allow where they are currently operating to hinder where they are going. In other words, it may be human nature for people to want the tree first, but all trees first begin with seeds.

Districts must also understand that there is not a one-size-fits-all or cookie-cutter model to which a school or district must adhere in order to become a bona fide PLO. PLOs should be customized to fit the unique needs of the organization; *no two PLO districts will look exactly the same*. On the other hand, PLOs should be willing to adhere to and invest in the following research-based core components of PLOs: a focus on student learning (e.g., guaranteed curriculum), a collaborative culture, and a results-oriented viewpoint.

The first step in becoming a PLO is to make the decision to get started. As U.S. author and physician Debasish Mridha once stated, "The secrets of success are getting started and being persistent." Districts should not wait until they have all the pieces to the puzzle to embark on the path of becoming a PLO. However, districts must be what Dr. Nick Osborne, professor of educational leadership at Eastern Illinois University, calls "consciously uninformed." To be consciously uninformed is to know what we do not know. If a district had the desire to become a PLO and was willing to learn what it did not know to become a PLO, this attitude of being consciously uninformed would increase that district's chances of becoming a successful PLO.

To successfully guide the district in becoming a PLO, it is vital that districts are sincere in their desire to create a collaborative governing and operational system for the district. For instance, it is disingenuous for districts to attempt to utilize PLOs as a guise for top-down governance with no authentic commitment genuinely to consider stakeholder input in regard to establishing district ends (e.g., mission, vision, values, and goals) and other major administrative and/or governance decisions. If stakeholders do not feel that the effort to collaborate is genuine, then trust will be violated, and the PLO cannot be implemented with fidelity.

This was evident when the superintendent of Florida's Palm Beach County District mandated collaborative teacher meetings. Because teachers saw this as a bureaucratic degree and top-down governance, the PLO model was not successful (Will, 2016). Trust is a cornerstone in order for effective systemic collaboration to take place, and stakeholders must all be willing to see mutual benefits in establishing a collaborative model.

After making the decision to invest in becoming a PLO, districts should evaluate where they are and what is needed to become a PLO and to begin the process of being "consciously uninformed." DuFour et al.'s book *Revisiting Professional Learning Communities at Work* provides an excellent continuum rubric that districts can utilize to measure their level of engagement or readiness in establishing, modifying, and/or sustaining a PLO (DuFour et al., 2008). DuFour's continuum rubric categorizes districts based on the following five stages:

- *Preinitiating*

  - There is no sense of district purpose, and improvement initiatives are fragmented.
  - Different individuals in the school system cannot agree on a course of action; there is competition to fund different pet projects.
  - Districts are discussing the PLO process and what is needed in order to have a successful implementation, such as district strategic planning to establish long-term goals of the organization (preparation stage; consultants may be warranted).

- *Initiating*

  - Leadership is somewhat clear about a unified direction, but the school system is unclear about district priorities. School/district leadership may have difficulty explaining district priorities.
  - Administrative actions are not in alignment with the stated plan regarding district initiatives.
  - Districts are beginning the process of implementing the PLO model (e.g., efforts are being made to begin transforming the district into a PLO).

- *Implementing*

  - District staff understand district ends (e.g., mission, vision, values, goals), but district buy-in is lacking.
  - District and school administrators have begun the process of implementing procedures that align with district ends. Staff who are not on board with district ends may be monitored and/or behaviors addressed.
  - Districts during this stage have successfully completed the first two stages and are developing systemic systems of collaboration and understanding; various staff members and other stakeholders are participating in the development and implementation of the district becoming a PLO.

- *Developing*

  - During this stage, districts have created systemic systems and are working to ensure that the PLO system is self-sustaining; structures are altered to support PLO changes and resources are devoted to ensuring the vitality of the PLO.
  - Members are receptive to the PLO and have experienced various benefits associated with the implementation of becoming a PLO. District staff members are changing their behavior to align with district expectations; staff are seeking additional resources to support district initiatives.

- *Sustaining*

  - During this stage, districts have established the process of how PLOs will function in their district (customized and unique to district needs), and internal and external stakeholders have a good understanding of the district's collaborative culture.
  - Policies, procedures, and structures are in place to sustain and evaluate the progress of district objectives (e.g., ongoing formative evaluations, annual summative evaluation, orientation programs for board members and staff members, professional development opportunities, and staff exit interviews).
  - The PLO becomes a way of life for the district and is the driving force behind all district work. The district's priorities are evident in the behavior of district staff members.
  - There are processes in place to celebrate success stories associated with the success of district initiatives.
  - Staff members not on board with district priorities are monitored and/or confronted.

To further the process of becoming a PLO, in what additional ways can districts become "consciously uninformed" or start the process of determining what they know and do not know about the PLO implementation process? How can districts evaluate where they are operating concerning the five stages of DuFour's continuum: preinitiating, initiating, implementing, developing, and sustaining? Districts must begin by collecting and analyzing data to lead their efforts or become results oriented. Districts may find that needs assessment surveys and/or other appraisal tools that align to the PLO continuum are helpful in collecting data to ensure that the district's alignment efforts are on target (Van Clay et al., 2011).

When establishing a PLO, the district must remember that ultimately it is attempting to influence district culture. Therefore, assessment surveys and/or other appraisal tools can assist the governance/administrative team in better understanding the present organizational climate or the shared perceptions and attitudes of the organization based on data. The governance/administrative team should heed the words of Arthur Conan Doyle, Scottish physician and historian, who said, "It is a capital mistake to theorize before one has data." In short, if the GLT fails to understand its current state by transforming data into knowledge and insight, the district cannot properly become a PLO.

Appraisal tools allow the district to collect data that is necessary to explain and to gain further insight and understanding about various ongoing conclusions made about the organization. The following appraisal tool can be used to survey district staff about districtwide PLO alignment initiatives and gauge approximately where the district is operating on the PLO continuum.

Instead of determining if a district is or is not a bona fide PLO according to educational pundits, a continuum is helpful in determining the district's current state and/or progress as a PLO. The appraisal tool measures alignment across the three big ideas of a PLO: a focus on learning, a focus on results, and a focus on collaboration.

The following appraisal tool (Figure 7.1) is based on a survey in *Learning by Doing* by DuFour, DuFour, Eaker, and Many (2006). The survey was designed to evaluate where the district or district school was on the PLO continuum and was broken into eight sections: focus, shared mission, collective commitments (shared values), purpose, communication, teaming, monitoring, and intervention.

Professional Learning Organization: A Sample of Needs Assessment

<u>Directions:</u> Please rate your district by circling your response. If an item does not apply, do not respond to it.
Rating Scale:

Strongly Disagree	Disagree	Undecided	Agree	Strongly Agree
(1)	(2)	(3)	(4)	(5)

Items	*Your Rating*
Focus on Learning (Questions 1-13) — A focus on learning entails what students should know and be able to do, and what assistance will be provided to students who have learning difficulties. The mantra of PLO districts is the belief that all students will achieve at high levels. A Focus on Learning entails a system of meaningful assessments and appropriate interventions to ensure student learning.	
1. The staff work together (e.g., teacher teams) to help ensure that students have a guaranteed and viable curriculum. This entails reaching a consensus about what students should know and be able to do based on a common curriculum and common standards that are age/grade appropriate. Teachers have been provided with a copy of district and/or state standards.	1 2 3 4 5
2. Multiple stakeholders (school board, administration, district staff, parents, and community members) work collaboratively to address student learning needs (e.g., district open houses, parent-teacher conferences, state of the district address to the community, teacher team meetings, and district team meetings).	1 2 3 4 5
3. District-wide benchmark assessments (e.g., formative and summative performance-based assessments; state and district assessments) are administered throughout the year to help guide the curriculum and to help determine if student learning has occurred.	1 2 3 4 5
4. Students know and understand what they are expected to know and understand.	1 2 3 4 5
5. District stakeholders, both internal and external (administration, community, parents, students, and teachers) are aware of the district's non-negotiable learning standards for student achievement and instruction.	1 2 3 4 5
6. Administration and staff trust and respect each other to work collaboratively to address student achievement concerns; our staff feels valued and respected.	1 2 3 4 5
7. No effort has been made by the district/school to establish improvement goals related to student learning.	1 2 3 4 5
8. Professional development is focused on student learning and/or on district goals. A variety of opportunities exists for collective learning.	1 2 3 4 5

Figure 7.1. PLO needs assessment

9. Teachers often work independently of each other and seldom work in teams; each teacher creates his/her own assessments to monitor student learning. The staff seldom work collaboratively to review student work.	1 2 3 4 5
10. The district/school does not encourage parental or community engagement regarding student learning.	1 2 3 4 5
11. There is a coordinated district/school response when students are not learning and/or meeting benchmarks; schools provide additional time and support for students who experience learning difficulties.	1 2 3 4 5
12. What happens when a student does not learn will depend almost exclusively on the classroom teacher. The school has no coordinated system of intervention for struggling students.	1 2 3 4 5
13. Opportunities exist for peer observations, coaching, and mentoring regarding instructional and other academic practices.	1 2 3 4 5
Focus on Results (Questions 14-26) — A focus on results encompasses: how district expectations (district goals) are being monitored, access to meaningful data, how issues are resolved, and how the district celebrates its successes. A focus on results centers on data management and staff having a data mindset on which their decisions are based.	
14. Staff members are beginning to see evidence of the benefits of clearly established expectations for student learning and systematic processes to monitor student learning.	1 2 3 4 5
15. The school board regularly discusses student achievement at board meetings.	1 2 3 4 5
16. Periodically the superintendent arranges for various district/school teams to provide academic updates to the school board regarding district and/or school priorities.	1 2 3 4 5
17. There is no alignment between district/school goals regarding student achievement outcomes.	1 2 3 4 5
18. The district/school celebrates district/school successes.	1 2 3 4 5
19. Staff members are committed to helping all students learn; staff (e.g., teacher teams) examines practices and procedures to measure the impact on student learning. The achievement of each student is monitored on a timely basis.	1 2 3 4 5
20. Teachers and administration work collaboratively while paying close attention to test assessment results and to ensure that processes are in place to help interpret student learning data.	1 2 3 4 5
21. Staff members are given meaningful evaluations to help aid their professional growth.	1 2 3 4 5
22. The district/school provides professional development regarding how to properly analyze and interpret data related to student-learning outcomes.	1 2 3 4 5

Figure 7.1 *(continued)*

23. Staff members are not aware of district goals or how district goals impact their work on a day-to-day basis. There is no universal understanding of the purpose and priorities of the district.	1	2	3	4	5
24. Periodically the staff discuss district and/or school systems and procedures to analyze what is working and what is not working; appropriate adjustments and/or recommendations are made based on these conversations.	1	2	3	4	5
25. Each teacher has access to various student data reports (e.g., test scores, learning rubrics) in order to gather evidence to determine if learning has occurred. The staff has accessibility to key information.	1	2	3	4	5
26. The school schedule is often an impediment for teachers working collaboratively; time is not provided for teachers to work in groups.	1	2	3	4	5
Focus on Collaboration (Questions 27-39) — A focus on collaboration entails how systemic collaboration and communication are fostered throughout the district to ensure organizational effectiveness (School Leadership for Results, 2015). A focus on collaboration centers on a collaborative culture and agreement and collaboration regarding district ends (e.g., shared values and beliefs, mission, vision, goals).					
27. The purpose and/or mission of the district/school have not been articulated. Most staff views the mission of the school as teaching. Leadership may understand the purpose, but people throughout the organization remain unclear. Seldom are there opportunities for the staff to initiate change.	1	2	3	4	5
28. Few people were involved in the creation of the district/school improvement plan and/or the strategic plan to formulate goals or priorities for the district/school. No effort has been made to engage staff and community in describing the preferred conditions for the district/school. The staff is consistently not involved in discussing and making decisions about the district/school.	1	2	3	4	5
29. The school has begun to alter the structures, resources and rewards to better align with district priorities. Efforts are made to ensure that the staff understands the direction of district schools and that all staff is on board with district priorities. Staff throughout the district is generally informed about what is occurring in school buildings other than their own.	1	2	3	4	5
30. Stakeholders (community, parents, students, teachers) are aware of the district/school priorities and those priorities are highly visible. Staff members can easily identify various target goals. Those priorities are frequently discussed at the school and district level.	1	2	3	4	5
31. Staff members are aware of the specific commitments needed on their part to advance the district and/or the school's purpose. Leaders confront incongruent behavior.	1	2	3	4	5
32. District ends (values and beliefs, mission, vision, and goals) are embraced by staff and embedded in the school's culture. Staff members realize the benefits of a PLO.	1	2	3	4	5
33. Staff feels overwhelmed by what they consider as a never-ending series of fragmented, disjointed, and short-lived improvement initiatives in which they have little or no input.	1	2	3	4	5
34. There is a general understanding of the purpose and priorities of the school, and	1	2	3	4	5

Figure 7.1 *(continued)*

collaborative teams are in place, but people throughout the organization remain unreceptive.					
35. Staff throughout the organization feels pressured to collaborate on what they see as top-down management priorities and feel as though they have no authentic collaborative input.	1	2	3	4	5
36. There are high-performing collaborative teams throughout the district that regularly meet (a representative from each group meeting together) and in separate groups for the purpose of advancing district/school priorities; there is a high degree of trust and respect among team members in part due to group behavioral norms to ensure collegial relationships.	1	2	3	4	5
37. New staff members are given an orientation to the district which includes mentoring to support staff stability.	1	2	3	4	5
38. When a staff member leaves the district, an exit interview is given to learn the reasons why a person was leaving the district and to promote staff stability.	1	2	3	4	5
39. The purpose and priorities of the school are evident by the everyday behavior of people throughout the school. Collaboration is seen as a way of life throughout the district. Decision-making takes place through various team committees.	1	2	3	4	5

Figure 7.1 *(continued)*

After learning where the district is on the PLO continuum, districts must begin the conversation as to how to move the district forward properly in its implementation of becoming a PLO relative to its given state. During this process, the administration should consider formulating a dashboard or action plan based on timelines of implementation. In drafting the action plan, the administration should consider how to respond to the five categories (preinitiating, initiating, implementing, developing, and sustaining) of the PLO continuum rubric (DuFour et al., 2006). Based on these five categories, the district should consider various indicators, initiatives, resources, and other evidence, such as:

- *Preinitiating* (During this stage there is no districtwide systemic process in place to improve district/school performance; improvement efforts may be disjointed.)

  - Is there a need for consultants to assist the district's efforts in becoming a PLO?
  - Is there a need for district strategic planning and/or setting district goals and direction? (If so, should the district work with a consultant?)
  - Is there a need for surveys and/or focus groups to gather information of stakeholders prior to establishing PLO initiatives?

- *Initiating* (The district has announced its intent to become a PLO; there is no structured program in place and staff may see this as another come-and-go initiative.)

  - When will a PLO action implementation plan be completed? Will it include timelines and indicators, and how will the action plan be monitored to ensure that the PLO is implemented with fidelity?

- When will priority goals that were identified in district strategic planning be agreed upon?

- *Implementing* (Administrators begin working with district staff to build shared knowledge and understanding about how the district's PLO will work and to build consensus; administrators provide resources for schools to operate as a PLO including time for team meetings and systems of interventions; administration monitors how the PLO is being implemented and addresses incongruent behaviors. Some schools may implement the PLO with various degrees of fidelity at this stage.)

  - How are systemic teams/systems of communication developed?
  - How are staff members monitored to ensure compliance?
  - How are professional development needs determined?
  - How is time allotted for team collaboration?

- *Developing* (Various PLO processes are in place; the governance, strategic, tactical, and operational teams all work interdependently to achieve common goals; issues are quickly analyzed and resolved.)

  - In what ways does the district/school celebrate success?
  - Formative/summative evaluations are completed, and appropriate changes are made to the PLO system.
  - What systems of communication are in place between various PLO teams throughout the district?

- *Sustaining* (There are high-performing PLO teams throughout the district that are all interconnected; PLO is seen as a way of life; there is a laser focus on student learning, all stakeholders feel valued and supported; stakeholders can identify the priorities of the district/school.)

  - During this stage, districts have established the process of how PLOs will function in their district (customized and unique to district needs), and internal and external stakeholders have a good understanding of the district's collaborative culture.
  - Policies, procedures, and structures are in place to sustain and evaluate the progress of district objectives (e.g., ongoing formative evaluations, annual summative evaluation, orientation programs for board members and staff members, professional development opportunities, and staff exit interviews).

It has been said that "what gets monitored, gets done," or perhaps we should say that it has a better chance of being completed. Typically when a new initiative is launched, there is a lot of excitement during the genesis stages. With time, the best programs fizzle out if the organization does not take time out to celebrate successes and, more importantly, to monitor the program continuously. During the sustaining stage, it cannot be overstated about the importance of the administrative teams establishing protocols regarding how the program will be evaluated. Additionally, it is important to discuss how new staff will be oriented to the PLO process, and to ensure that staff exit interviews are completed.

It is imperative that evaluations take place so that the district can be proactive in identifying factors that lead to successful implementation, as well as factors detrimental to the PLO process. Concerning orientation programs, the district leaders must remember that they are striving to create and sustain a collaborative culture, and a major cornerstone to establishing that culture is the proper orientation and induction of individuals.

Furthermore, it is equally vital for administration to conduct exit interviews of staff. Exit interviews allow administrators an opportunity to engage in courageous conversations with staff who may be more open to sharing their honest opinions since they are leaving the district.

Preinitiating, initiating, implementing, developing, and sustaining are five crucial stages in implementing and sustaining a successful PLO. Administrators must be cautious in developing appropriate appraisal tools as well as formulating action plans for successful implementation. Again, administrators need to understand the culture of the district properly and have a good understanding where the district is currently operating prior to charting any new directions.

When a PLO is being implemented, the governance team must be of one accord. The school board and the superintendent must be a good fit and equally value the concept of collaborative governance and systems of communication among stakeholders. It is the job of the school board to clarify the district's purpose (mission and vision), and it is the job of the superintendent to implement that purpose on behalf of the school board. If the school board or the superintendent does not equally value collaborative governance, then the PLO cannot be implemented with fidelity.

How can school boards help identify superintendents who believe in collaboration? And why is this important? As noted, PLOs cannot be implemented with fidelity if there is no buy-in from the chief executive officer or the superintendent. Moreover, if governance teams hire a superintendent who does not agree with the direction of the board, then boards may have to pay substantial compensation if they hope to void the superintendent's contract. According to Superville (2017), districts of all sizes have awarded lucrative financial packages to superintendents in exchange for resignations or retirements with some districts spending upwards of $1.65 million in severance packages.

Below are some sample interview questions school boards may want to consider asking potential superintendent applicants to gauge their views regarding collaborative governance.

SAMPLE SUPERINTENDENT INTERVIEW QUESTIONS FOR THOSE DISTRICTS SEEKING A COLLABORATIVE LEADER

Note: These are sample questions only; the ideal candidate may be unaware of systemic collaborative school systems. Therefore, you are attempting to gauge his or her willingness to work collaboratively and to learn how to implement a systemic collaborative system. If the applicant is willing, the board should be willing to support professional development initiatives.

1. What are your thoughts about top-down management (in which direction comes from the governance team and staff is told to comply) approaches as well as bottom-up management approaches such as site-based schools?

   How do you define collaborative leadership, and do you agree with its concepts? If so, can you give some examples of how you would use collaborative leadership to lead the district?

   Are you aware of the concept of professional learning communities (PLCs)? If so, how would you describe a PLC school/district?

   a. Do you embrace PLC concepts of focus on learning, results, and collaboration? Why or why not?

2. Do you believe that the board should occasionally hear from multiple stakeholders (directed by the superintendent but is a board expectation) in an effort to better understand student achievement and organizational effectiveness? Or should the board rely solely on its superintendent for information regarding district operations?

3. Are you willing to promote collaborative relationships between the superintendent and other administrators, administration, and operational staff, and are you willing to promote greater collaboration between the district, its schools, and various community stakeholders?

   a. Can you provide examples of how you will promote these collaborative relationships?

   b. What are your thoughts about teacher-led team meetings via grade and/or department?

4. Can you describe the ideal relationship between the school board and its superintendent?

5. What do you see as the role of the superintendent in promoting professional development for the school board?
6. How would you ensure that the board is informed about district programs and is knowledgeable about what is occurring in district schools?
7. It is the job of the school board to formulate a strategic plan, but what are your thoughts regarding how such a plan should be formulated?

The governance and administrative team in particular must realize that no matter how hard it tries, not all staff members may be receptive to being a part of a collaborative culture. The key for the administrative team is to ensure that it has the appropriate people leading the various teams, since leadership starts from the top. Jim Collins (2001), author of *Good to Great*, provided some sound practical advice that administrative teams should consider in implementing and/or sustaining a PLO. Collins suggested that administrators continuously ask the question, "First who, then what?" Collins believes that successful business leaders of successful companies go from "good to great" by not starting with the "where" but with the "who."

Collins (2001) described his concept of "first who, then what" by comparing a business to a bus and the leader to a bus driver. Successful leaders, in an effort to ensure that the organization is not at a standstill, have to determine where the organization is going, how it will get there, and who is going with them. In short, good leaders start with people first and then establish direction (collaborative leadership). Therefore, leaders must ensure that the right people are on the bus, the right people are in their seats, and the wrong people are off the bus. Based on this analogy, Collins (2001) suggested the following steps:

1. Get the right people on the bus.

   - Leaders must have a good evaluation and selection process for staff members (e.g., observations, feedback, interviews, references, background checks, testing)

2. Get the right people in the right seats.

   - Attempt to have all key seats (positions) filled with the right people; leadership starts from the top. Note that all seats do not have to have the right people, but the key seats are vital.

3. Get the wrong people off the bus.

- For individuals who are the wrong fit for the district's culture, assist them to leave with dignity, grace, and self-respect. It is important that the remaining staff view the organization positively.

4. Put "who" before "what."

   - When the organization encounters a problem or an opportunity, instead of asking the "what" question or "What should we do?," ask the "who" question, or "Who is the right person to take responsibility for this?"
   - Organizations must spend the bulk of their time investing in human capital and/or people decisions.

Superintendent Chrostoski agrees with the premise of Collins. In 2017, she stated that

> the journey of this district embracing the philosophy of professional learning communities has been slow and steady. Although much research is out there on the success of the PLC process in individual buildings, a district system's approach is not so common. . . . Goshen County S.D. #1 is committed to preparing each student to become a career- and college-ready citizen.
>
> . . .When the district decided to embrace the PLC process, we knew there would be challenges because of the geography, but felt creating collegial teams for all 1st grade teachers, 3rd grade teachers, Algebra 1 teachers, etc., was the only way for our district to provide each student with a guaranteed and viable curriculum. . . . Switching from teachers working in isolation to working together to design common curriculum and assessments can be intimidating and uncomfortable for some. It is a tremendous amount of work and those involved have to be willing to take risks and endure failure. It has taken the district four years to change the culture. This also meant getting the right people on the bus and encouraging others to find a new one.
>
> . . .To say that we have seen a sudden growth in student achievement would not be accurate. We are seeing pockets of greatness in the district and with that knowledge can now share with each other what works and what doesn't. (J. Chrostoski, personal communication, October 3, 2017)

Chapter Eight

School Board Leadership and Superintendent Leadership Are Essential

SCHOOL BOARD LEADERSHIP

School boards must properly understand their authority and influence and use that knowledge in an appropriate way to maximize student achievement. School boards can change culture by properly understanding and governing in their strategic role as opposed to the tactical and operational role of staff. Traditionally, there has been a lot of confusion regarding how school boards impact student achievement and how to hold the school system properly accountable for student learning. If school boards govern by the principles outlined in this book, they can change district culture. School boards must always remember that leadership starts from the top.

Most school boards often would like to do a better job in ensuring that their school system is transparent and maintains open communications with all of its stakeholders, but most do not know where to start. This book is essential in helping governance teams get off first base with this task. School board members as trustees for their communities know and understand that a school system built on collaboration and shared leadership is vital in enhancing student learning as evident with Goshen County S.D. #1.

Under the leadership of Superintendent Chrostoski, the 2016–2017 Wyoming PAWS (Proficiency Assessments for Wyoming) data revealed that Goshen County S.D. #1 is above the state average in many academic areas, such as reading and math for various grades (J. Chrostoski, personal communication, October 3, 2017). The governance team attributed this success to their PLO system based on collaboration and on shared leadership.

The School District of Menomonee Falls, Wisconsin, made front-page headlines in *Education Week* in February 2018 for continuous improvement strategies that incorporated PLO tenets. Specifically, in the past six years, the district went from a low-performing status based on federal guidelines to become one of the top-performing school districts in the state of Wisconsin (Sparks, 2018b). Ironically, the district managed to become a top-performing school district while confronted with declining state revenues and changes in administrative leadership.

What was the key to Menomonee Falls' success? First, the school board showed leadership by desiring change. As previously noted, leadership must start from the top. The school board desired data-driven decision-making and to get off the pendulum swing of trying various packaged reforms in a search to find the perfect fix for the district's woes. The first major decision of the school board was to hire a superintendent who believed in collaborative governance and continuous improvement (Sparks, 2018b). As already mentioned, if the superintendent does not believe in collaborative leadership/governance and the vision of the board, it is doubtful that PLOs will flourish.

The School District of Menomonee Falls was successful because the board consciously changed the district's culture by making sure everyone shared the workload. The superintendent was charged with creating systems of communication between the school board, bus drivers, cafeteria workers, administrators, parents, students, and teachers in order for stakeholders to help share the workload (Sparks, 2018b). The district's focus on collaborative governance yielded the following benefits:

- An increase in student attendance
- An increase in advanced placement classes
- An improvement in Community engagement
- An increase in student math scores
- A decrease in student suspensions
- A decrease in worker compensation claims
- Professional development for all staff

School improvement measures that do not rely on collaboration are seldom if ever successful. This includes state and national reform efforts that have led to overhauling educator evaluation systems and making it more rigorous for individuals to become educators. This also includes the belief that one dynamic administrator can turn around a school and/or a district. Districts that rely on punitive measures and/or top-down measures to force change, such as the turnaround models of school reform promoted by former secretary of education Arne Duncan, will not succeed. Carbaugh et al. (2015) noted:

What we are learning from our new evaluation systems, as district after district struggles with rapid implementation and all the bumps and slides that installing new system entails, is that first of all, change is hard. In fact, without the cooperation and committed collaboration of the majority of stakeholders in the system, and without a shared focus, common goals, and agreement about best practices, change is not just hard; it's impossible.

Secretary Duncan promoted failed school turnaround models that included concepts such as forcing schools to convert to charter schools and closing down low-performing schools, replacing the principal and at least half of the teaching staff, and promoting merit pay systems (Klein, 2013).

According to Klein, Shawnee High School in Louisville, Kentucky, utilized the turnaround model of school reform with disastrous results. In alignment with a turnaround model of school reform, Shawnee High School relocated half of its teaching staff and received support from Kentucky's veteran educators, relocated veteran principal Keith Look from a successful high-performing middle school, received a School Improvement Grant (SIG) of $1.5 million, and recruited superstar teachers from other district schools.

After sinking in tremendous resources along with positive remarks by Arne Duncan showcasing the power of School Improvement Grants and turnaround models of school reforms, Shawnee High School failed to improve, leading the onetime superstar principal Keith Look to submit his letter of resignation (Klein, 2013). What is the difference between Shawnee and Menomonee Falls? The difference is that Menomonee Falls chose collaboration and shared leadership as opposed to top-down governance approaches. As DuFour, DuFour, and Eaker (2008) insisted, collaboration and shared leadership (e.g., creating professional learning communities) is the only promising strategy for continuous improvement.

As evident with Menomonee Falls, it is doubtful that any school or district improvement initiative will be successful if it is not endorsed and supported by the school board. Superintendent Chrostoski noted the importance of the board's role in its district's PLO process when she stated that

> the board's role in the success of our story has been instrumental. Members have undergone training with Solution Tree and have supported the professional development of its teachers with acclaimed educators, experts and researchers to include Mike Mattos, Anthony Muhammad, Ken Williams, Tim Brown, Ken O'Connor, Thomas Guskey, and Louis Cruz. . . . Our board of education sets aside board meeting time and designates two board work sessions a year JUST to look at student data and hear from the curriculum director, principals and teachers on what methodologies they will change and what interventions will be used to assure that all students achieve to high levels. . . . No district can be high achieving unless it has a high-achieving board of education. As superintendent, it is my job to provide them with the information, professional development, and the evidence they need to know that we

ARE providing the best possible learning and educational environment for our students. Only a courageous board can be at the helm, because as the culture begins to change, staff will leave and new teachers will come on board who will need mentoring and support to transition into the work we do. (J. Chrostoski, personal communication, October 3, 2017)

Again, good governance must start from the top. School boards must play a crucial role in determining district ends (e.g., mission, vision, values and beliefs, goals) and codifying board expectations in district policy. Furthermore, the school board must be able to communicate its vision for the district while empowering the superintendent to bring that vision into reality. Former consultant for the California School Boards Association D'Karla Assagai agrees and noted:

> School boards have a tremendous role in making decisions on behalf of the entire community that affect the education of each student in their districts. The role of the board should represent the community's voice and provide governance in education that considers every child's best interests. Boards also have the responsibility to oversee and work with their only employee: the superintendent. Effective school boards balance managing, partnering, and supporting the superintendent to shift resources that support all students to ensure that the district's goals are achieved. With all that is at stake, it is critical for a school board to clearly identify its expectations and set those standards in board policy. Not only does this practice offer transparency in the board's intention but it also holds them accountable to those standards. Codifying expectations in board policy sets the tone for the board and serves as a measure from which they should govern. (D. Assagai, personal communication, June 7, 2018)

School boards can impact student achievement, and the manner in which the school board does its work matters to the overall success of the district.

As with the theme of this book, it takes a systemic, collaborative approach to operate the district successfully and to foster student improvement continuously. As noted by Martin and Rains (2018), no one can lead alone because the responsibilities of running a school district in areas such as pedagogy, instruction, assessment, curriculum, technology, research, and data analysis are simply too great for one individual.

This is why leaders must lead using the collaborative governance approach, which recognizes and utilizes the strengths of various individuals to reach common goals and to encourage other individuals to become leaders as well (Martin & Rains, 2018). Also, it enables the leaders to influence others effectively in meeting organizational goals. As noted by leadership guru John Maxwell (2001), "Leadership is about influence, nothing more and nothing less."

Unfortunately, too many educational reforms have placed too much focus on a single educational leader such as the principal to be the linchpin in improving learning conditions of schools rather than relying on collaborative PLO (Martin & Rains, 2018). For instance, Chicago public school principals are being empowered and used as the essential key to turn around Chicago city schools (Sparks, 2018a).

According to research by the University of Chicago Consortium on School Research, principals are effective not by utilizing top-down management approaches but by focusing on building a collaborative culture. Successful principals are those who invest in professional learning communities such as TLTs (as cited in Sparks, 2018a).

Superintendent Dr. Nathaniel Cunningham Jr., superintendent of Thornton Township High School District 205, agrees with collaborative governance and has stated:

> We have known since Rosenholtz's book was published in 1989, *Teacher's Workplace: The Social Organization of Schools*, that schools can only be successful with the support of school districts. The belief that educational leaders, regardless of their knowledge and skills, could move schools single-handedly remains a fallacy among some educational pundits. Principal leadership is key; however effective principals must rally their staff in a collaborative manner and rely on the support of the school district to ultimately be successful in carrying out the aims of the organization. PLCs can only exist with the support of the district. Therefore, schools must be viewed as nested layers of districts because schools cannot and do not support themselves. (N. Cunningham, personal communication, July 17, 2018)

Dr. Cunningham's belief about principal leadership is supported by educational researchers such as Robert J. Marzano. Carbaugh et al.'s (2015) book titled *School Leadership for Results: Shifting the Focus of Leader Evaluation* stated the following about the dual leadership role of principals:

> The school leader has always stood as the man or woman with a foot in both worlds—the person with direct personal connections to teachers, students, and parents, on the one hand, and who is accountable to district leaders and board members, on the other. The school leader is a buffer and fulcrum, translator and adviser—the transformationalist who takes the dreams and challenges of policy and makes them practicable in real, working classrooms.

SUPERINTENDENT LEADERSHIP

Superintendents, as chief executive officers (CEOs) of the district, must realize that leadership is essential but only if they are practicing collaborative leadership. Why is this the case? As noted, the superintendent cannot lead a school district alone. It is the job of the superintendent to help grow the organization as discussed in Chapter 1.

The superintendent is arguably the face of the district, and therefore it is imperative for the superintendent to model what collaborative leadership looks like to influence staff properly and to engage the community in addressing organizational needs. If the superintendent fails to model collaborative leadership, various stakeholders may see the district's efforts to create a PLO as disingenuous and therefore may not buy-in or support the district's efforts.

As CEO of the district, it is the job of the superintendent to oversee the day-to-day operations of the district, which entail guiding, motivating, and monitoring district staff members. To role-model collaborative leadership effectively, the superintendent must exhibit trust, integrity, empathy, accessibility, and humility because he or she sets the tone for how other district administrators will work with staff members (Martin & Rains, 2018).

Trust is vital because it is an important factor in determining how staff members (such as teachers) will collaborate with district administrators. When trust is low, it is common for administrators to rely on power as an influencer rooted in top-down management styles. Integrity (e.g., honesty, commitment, consistency), which is a component of trust, is also important; staff need to know that they can trust district administrators (Martin & Rains, 2018).

Superintendents must role-model empathy or being mindful of human needs such as support and motivation. The superintendent must be mindful not to focus too much on data to the point that he or she fails to see people as people and thus fails to properly build relationships. Also, the superintendent must model what it means to be accessible. The superintendent can demonstrate caring by being visible and genuinely attentive to staff needs. Finally, superintendents should model humility. They can do this by the manner in which they handle errors and other mistakes (Martin & Rains, 2018). Instead of covering up or casting blame, effective superintendents take ownership for their mistakes and work to resolve issues.

As the CEO, the superintendent influences the behaviors of district staff members including having a direct impact on how other district administrators will work with district staff members. As noted earlier, leadership starts from the top. Superintendent leadership is essential in implementing the PLO with fidelity. As discussed previously, it is essential that the school board and the superintendent be a good fit and equally value the concept of collaborative decision-making, or else the PLO could never be implemented effectively.

Superintendent leadership is essential in the role that community engagement plays in enhancing the school district's organizational culture based on systemic collaboration with external stakeholders.

Chapter Nine

The Final Reason Why Districts Should Choose to Become PLOs

There are myriad reasons why school boards and superintendents should invest in establishing PLO systems. A key strength of PLO districts is that they enhance board–superintendent relationships by creating an organization that keeps all stakeholders focused on agreed-upon district ends (e.g., mission, vision, values and beliefs, goals) as compared to personal agendas. Furthermore, it is a system that delineates the role and duties between the board and its superintendent.

PLOs are customized to meet the needs of the district; therefore, PLOs can meet the needs of any district, regardless of demographics. Goshen County S.D. #1 achieved great success although the rural community presented challenges. Superintendent Chrostoski illustrated this when discussing her district's demographics:

> Goshen County S.D. #1 is no different than any other rural district in the United States, except for the challenge of its geography. Covering approximately 2,200 square miles and almost 1.5 million acres, it is ranked #1 in agricultural importance to the state's economy. That being said, covering so many miles and acres, the population hovers at a mere 13,300. The school district itself has 1,730 students, in seven buildings at four different communities. Other statistics include 400 certified and classified employees, 33 bus routes, ranging from 12 miles to 146 miles, with 1,100 students riding daily. (J. Chrostoski, personal communication, October 3, 2017)

PLOs will work for any size district, although there may be challenges and nuances. Common challenges include how to establish TLTs for schools when there may be only one grade level, or one classroom per grade level. Due to this issue, some districts have formed intrateams (e.g., different-grade-level teachers composing a team). Also, districts may find it easier to implement learning teams at the elementary school as opposed to the middle and high school due to the arrangement of more complicated student and staff scheduling.

The bottom line is that issues will arise and these will pose new challenges for the tactical (administrative) team in implementing a systemic PLO approach. Nevertheless, there are always solutions to problems. As Albert Einstein observed, "The significant problems we face cannot be solved at the same level of thinking we were at when we created them." Or as Edwin Louis Cole, founder of Christian Men's Network, stated, "You don't drown by falling into the water; you drown by staying there."

Districts may want to consider the vast resources available through organizations such as Solution Tree and networking and/or partnering with other successful PLO school districts to help overcome implementation challenges. This could provide districts with an opportunity to provide support systems for single-grade-level teachers, as well as a venue to exchange ideas and other resources.

Underlining the fact that a PLO is the only promising strategy for continuous improvement of school districts (DuFour et al., 2008), PLOs are based on sound research and are parallel to the internationally acclaimed kaizen continuous improvement model, referred to as kaizen. What is kaizen? Kaizen originated in Japan, and the word translates to mean "change (*kai*) for the good (*zen*)." Kaizen is grounded in the philosophical belief that everything can be enhanced and improved (MindTools, n.d.).Tradition or the belief in "business as usual" is a foreign idea for those who embrace this principle.

Kaizen was introduced as part of the Marshall Plan after World War II when U.S. occupying forces brought in experts to assist with the rebuilding of Japanese industry. As a part of the improvement plan, Civil Communications Section (CCS) taught statistical control methods as taught by great innovators such as W. Edwards Deming (MindTools, n.d.). The Economic and Scientific Section (ESS) group was instrumental in bringing pioneer Lowell Mellen (recommended by Deming and others) to install the Training Within Industry program that sought to improve Japanese management skills. This program focused on job instruction, job methods, and job relations, and transformed into what we now call kaizen (MindTools, n.d.).

Several companies have utilized kaizen; however, the Toyota Production System is the best-known example, in which all employees are expected to halt the production line if they deem that something may be abnormal with the product. After stopping the production line, employees are expected and encouraged to suggest improvements, which may evolve into future kaizens (improvements) (MindTools, n.d.).

Why is the kaizen model important? Toyota learned that when employees are empowered, it leads to higher job satisfaction and more quality products.

Toyota deemed that it is the employees who know the products the best and therefore should have an opportunity to give feedback regarding how products should be improved. According to MindTools (n.d.), Toyota experienced several other benefits of using kaizen, such as:

- Less waste; employee skills are used more efficiently.
- Job satisfaction significantly increases.
- Improved commitment; employees are more vested in their jobs.
- Improved retention; employee attrition decreases as employees have more of a stake in their jobs.
- Improved consumer satisfaction; higher-quality products with fewer errors.
- Improved problem solving; allows employees to be involved in discovering solutions from problems that may occur at the workplace.
- Improved teams; working together to solve problems builds greater unity.

As a result of using the kaizen model, in 2009 Toyota surpassed General Motors (GM) in number of overall vehicles sold and thus ended GM's 77-year reign as the world's number one auto manufacturer. As Toyota was experiencing this growth, in 1984 GM and Toyota agreed to work together at a car factory in Freemont, California. GM needed Toyota's expertise for building smaller cars, while Toyota needed GM's expertise with the U.S. market. The joint car factory was called NUMMI (New United Motor Manufacturing Incorporated) (Vocoli, 2014).

As part of the agreement, GM union workers trained for 2 weeks in Japan on Toyota's assembly line. When they worked for Toyota, GM workers were astounded by the collaboration between Toyota assembly workers and management. According to one GM assembly worker:

> At some point, somebody would come over and say, do you want me to help? And that was a revelation, because nobody in the GM plant would ever ask to help. They would come yell at you because you got behind. . . . [Our American work team] couldn't believe that responsiveness. I can't remember any time in my working life where anybody asked for my ideas to solve the problem. And they literally want to know, and when I tell them, they listen, and then suddenly, they disappear and somebody comes back with the tool that I just described—it's built—and they say, "Try this." (Vocoli, 2014)

When the American assembly workers returned from Japan to the NUMMI plant in California, they delivered equally powerful results. Prior to the joint collaboration, GM union workers at the plant had a reputation of being difficult to manage. According to Vocoli (2014), in less than 3 months the following occurred:

- The plant produced cars at near-perfect ratings that yielded various cost savings.
- GM workers earned a good reputation.
- One study concluded that it would cost GM 50% more labor to produce similar cars.
- Employee grievances and absenteeism were significantly reduced.

Toyota and GM learned that employee suggestions matter. According to Process Improvement Japan (n.d.), executive vice president Yasuhito Yamauchi (2005–2009) of Toyota noted the importance of his company adopting kaizen improvement methods when he stated:

> Actually, it's front line workers' ideas and suggestions which must be absorbed into the upper levels of management. Kaizen implementation is truly a bottom-up approach to effective management. In the West, there is a separation between blue collar and white collar workers. If blue collar workers must follow white collar rules, it inhibits effective kaizen, employee engagement and employee motivation—this inhibits cost reduction and profit maximization.

He also said:

> Unless we have vitalized front line workers, we cannot be successful. They are the ones who actually produce the product and the profit. Our job in management is to make them energized. . . . As a leader, I have to communicate the corporate vision to all members of the company and must show that we are very concerned about our vision and our future direction. Whenever I have time, I visit the Gemba [the real place, the place where the actual work is done] of all divisions. I visit people. Because I am in a high position, if I call others to come, it's no good. No, I go to them.

According to Enna (2013), there are lessons we can learn from Toyota regarding public education that fortunately PLOs incorporate, such as:

- Relationships with immediate supervisors. Administrators in PLO organizations simply do not give orders hoping to achieve various metrics. All stakeholders, such as teachers, administrators, and the school board are viewed as partners; this leads to more personal and enjoyable relationships.
- Belief in senior leadership. In PLOs like in kaizen workplaces, administrators are part of the business rather than detached supervisors. Administrators understand the problems that teachers and other professionals encounter. Also, teachers are involved in the school and/or district improvement process.

- Pride in working for the company. Like kaizen employees, teachers take an active role in their work environment and feel comfortable speaking to administrators when things go wrong. This enables educators to take pride in their work. In a PLO system, stakeholders work with their leaders rather than for them.

As PLO organizations know all too well, when employees are empowered and treated as experts, the following results occur:

- Job satisfaction increases (e.g., fewer absence days are used).
- Student achievement soars.
- There is less waste (employee skills are used effectively, and schools end their dependency upon canned educational improvement programs).
- Commitment and retention improve.
- Consumer (parent) satisfaction improves.
- Problem solving and teamwork among educators improves.

U.S. public educators do not need more canned curriculum programs or directives from politicians and/or reformers, many of whom have never set foot inside a classroom. Our educators need to be empowered and treated as the professionals. Our educators need a voice in determining what works to improve student achievement, especially since teachers are the ones closest to students.

A key reason why we have not seen continuous long-term improvement from programs such as No Child Left Behind (NCLB) and Race to the Top (RTT) is that these programs were based on top-down approaches. When we fail to engage stakeholders who are closest to students and mandate top-down improvements from politicians and/or reformers, it leads to adverse results such as the following:

- The people doing the work do not become engaged problem solvers but merely "order takers."
- The improvement may lead to "change," but not true systemic, ongoing improvement.
- The improvement is often resisted because its vital stakeholders had no involvement in its design or implementation.

Administrators or school boards may be hesitant to implement a PLO system because they are concerned about the need to be in control of the organization. When PLOs are properly executed, governance team members must remember that together they approve district ends and other nonnegotiables of the school district. In a PLO, the governance team is simply agreeing to give meaningful voice to stakeholders. This entails giving employees a certain degree of control, but the control is given with clearly defined boundaries, which the GLT sets and monitors.

GLTs must understand that all employees need a certain degree of control in order for employees to become engaged and for their work not to be deemed as mundane. As Karen Martin, author of *The Outstanding Organization* , noted: " The people who do the work are the experts, not leaders nor consultants. If you want employees to engage, you must create the conditions for engagement to occur" (Martin, n.d.).

Various educational reformers have sought to incorporate business concepts such as charter schools, vouchers, and merit pay, all rooted in free-market concepts such as competition, as antidotes to public education woes. Researchers have discovered that following business precepts rooted in competition does not improve public education in a systemic and continuous manner. Despite this fact, many educational reformers are constantly on the lookout to determine how they can incorporate business concepts into public education.

The kaizen continuous improvement model is a proven business model and is similar to the PLO model because both are based on collaboration and human relationships as compared to competitive business approaches. Reformers who love to incorporate business models into public education should promote PLOs because of the commonalities with an effective business model.

As noted, PLOs are based on sound research practices and also serve as catalysts for meeting ESSA (Every Student Succeeds Act) guidelines. What is ESSA? According to the U.S. Department of Education (n.d.), ESSA replaced No Child Left Behind (NCLB) on December 10, 2015, and seeks to improve student and school success. Some of the highlights of the ESSA educational law include:

• It promotes equity for America's disadvantaged and high-need students.
• It requires students be taught using high academic standards that will lead to college and/or a career.
• It ensures that meaningful information (e.g., assessments aligned to standards) is provided to all stakeholders (e.g., educators, families, students, and communities).
• It supports local innovations—including evidence-based and place-based interventions by educators and other stakeholders.

ESSA requires each state to submit a customized accountability plan to the federal Department of Education for approval. ESSA allows for each state to set its own goals and measurements of student progress regarding academic outcomes, including school quality and student success. Furthermore, the law ensures that states take significant steps to narrow academic proficiency gaps that may exist with any subgroup (U.S. Department of Education, n.d.).

As noted, PLOs can be used to meet a variety of ESSA expectations, such as the highlights listed above. To further determine how PLOs could align to ESSA benchmarks, let's examine the Illinois State Board of Education (ISBE) Quality Framework for Illinois School Districts. According to ISBE (n.d.), the Illinois framework is a guide for districts that seeks to improve school quality and student success by focusing on the following seven researched standards:

1. Continuous Improvement
2. Culture and Climate
3. Shared Leadership
4. Governance
5. Education and Employee Quality
6. Family and Community Connections
7. Student and Learning Development

Below is a description of each Illinois standard, along with indicators, and suggestions on how the PLO could align to these standards (ISBE, n.d.). Chapter 3 provides further information regarding the roles and duties of PLC teams.

Standard I—Continuous Improvement

In successful districts and schools, there is a collective commitment to collaboratively identify, plan, implement, monitor, evaluate, and communicate the changes necessary to improve student learning continuously.

Indicator A—Focused and Coherent Direction

The district leadership team establishes a coherent and collaborative approach for improving student performance by relying on a continuous improvement process plan (e.g., established vision/goals).

PLO Alignment

- The governance learning team (note: GLT is synonymous with the district leadership team utilized by ISBE) ensures collaborative goal setting (formulation of district ends: mission, vision, values, and district goals—collaborative leadership/governance) that encompasses various internal and external stakeholders (e.g., administration, teachers, parents, students, business owners).

- Systematic processes to achieve goals (SMART goals)
- Utilize multiple data sets to improve student learning and monitor district ends
- Promote equity because it is based upon multiple internal/external stakeholders

- Guarantee systems of communications and input that encompass all district stakeholders (internal and external) and monitor the level of trust between the district and its schools.
- Establish nonnegotiable goals for student achievement and instruction.
- Help clarify and monitor what students are to learn.
- Ensure systems for capacity building (e.g., orientation of new hires, exit interviews, succession planning).
- District ends are codified in board policies and in administrative procedures.

Indicator B—Processes and Structure

The school(s) leadership team establishes a well-defined structure for building professional relationships and processes necessary to engage all school-level stakeholders.

PLO Alignment

Note: The BLT is synonymous with the school leadership team used by ISBE.

- Coordinating all-staff building meetings to (collaboratively):

  - Clarify the school's purpose and/or mission
  - Develop a school improvement plan (ensure the plan is linked to district ends)
  - Create a sense of urgency concerning district/school priorities and engage in collaborative problem solving

- Developing communication procedures

  - Internal/external stakeholder communications (school–community relations, teacher–parent communications, parent groups, and staff protocols for dealing with issues)

- Overseeing building TLT/support staff teams (e.g., focus on student learning)

- Ensuring that the collaborative team's mission is clear and concise (focus on learning, collaborative culture, focus on results)
- Providing appropriate resources to learning teams
- Providing assistance with how to interpret data

- Assisting in planning a guaranteed and viable curriculum (focus on learning)

  - Providing assistance with federal, state, or local student assessments
  - Ensuring that teachers are provided copies of various learning standards and assisting in soliciting staff input regarding the district's curriculum guide
  - Ensuring that staff know and understand how to "unpack" learning standards
  - Providing resources to struggling learners and those who meet or exceed learning expectations
  - Formative and summative assessments are used to guide instructional strategies.

- Assisting with staff professional development needs

  - New teachers are mentored.
  - Staff development is maintained.

Indicator C—Monitoring for Results

The district and school leadership teams collaboratively monitor changes in practice and implement adjustments, evaluate the results of student learning, and communicate the progress to all stakeholders.

PLO Alignment

The GLT and BLT teams (e.g., ISBE's district leadership and school leadership teams, respectively) regularly monitor the implementation of district ends including any necessary adjustments that need to be made. To ensure transparency, stakeholders are kept current in several ways such as district and school newsletters, websites, and through social media.

The GLT and BLT teams regularly communicate in two-way conversations in a variety of ways, such as communicating with each other at scheduled board meetings and through participating in the DLT (see Chapter 5). DLT representatives, such as school DLT representatives, can share information learned with members of their respective schools, which will provide an awareness of what is occurring throughout the district. Sharing of information is necessary in order to build relationships throughout the district and to generate the belief that district stakeholders are working collaboratively to meet organizational goals as opposed to operating as individual school units.

Standard II—Culture and Climate

In order to ensure desired results of improved teaching and learning, successful districts and schools must cultivate safe and stabilized learning environments.

Indicator A—Shared Vision and Goals

The district and school(s) have aligned vision statements and goals that support a learning environment that is physically, socially, emotionally, and behaviorally safe and conducive to learning.

PLO Alignment

- PLO organizations ensure that district and school ends or the mission, vision, values and beliefs, and goals of the district are aligned.
- The district learning team (DLT), which is composed of various representatives (such as district school teacher leaders, principals, central office, board members, and community members), meets periodically to ensure that district stakeholders support district ends and are implementing district ends with fidelity.
- The DLT helps to ensure that there is a positive districtwide learning environment that seeks to influence district culture positively, which, in turn, positively impacts stakeholder behaviors. This includes a focus on creating a safe learning environment for all district schools.

Indicator B—High Expectations for All

The school culture supports educators in practicing effective and responsive instruction to meet the needs of the whole child and promotes the celebration of district, school, and student improvement.

PLO Alignment

- It is the ultimate duty of the GLT to make sure the school district has a laser focus on learning, results, and collaboration. These areas constitute the fundamental aims of the PLO.
- The GLT holds the ALT led by the superintendent responsible for ensuring that staff utilizes evidence-based instruction, culturally responsive instruction, and that district, school, and student improvement is always celebrated.

- The GLTs are kept apprised of student instruction initiatives and monitoring data to ensure student achievement and that student successes are being celebrated accordingly.

Indicator C — Safe and Engaging Environments

The district and school climate supports the whole child and well-being of all students and personnel, contributing to an engaging and inclusive learning community.

PLO Alignment

- A key purpose of the PLO is to promote a district and school climate that caters to the physical, cultural, and socioeconomic needs of all students based on collaboration of internal and external stakeholders.
- PLO seeks to positively influence the organizational culture, which reflects the values, beliefs, and norms that characterize an organization as a whole.
- In PLO districts, various stakeholders such as administrators, board members, parents, students, teachers, and other stakeholders frequently spend time and collaborate, which fosters a natural propensity to develop a common set of expectations.
- Collaboration between PLO teams such as GLTs and TLTs will minimize the "us-versus-them" mentality.
- Collaboration of stakeholders fosters an engaged and inclusive learning community.

Standard III — Shared Leadership

In successful districts and schools, leaders create and sustain organizational direction, expectations, and a system that promotes excellence, efficiency, and leadership from within.

Indicator A — Administrative Leadership

The administration actively models and fosters a positive learning environment in which staff members feel valued and are challenged to be engaged and to grow professionally.

PLO Alignment

It is the duty of the ALT led by the superintendent to oversee all operations of the district. A major duty of the ALT is to ensure that there is a system in place that will yield a high degree of collaboration among all stakeholders and especially between administrators and teachers. The collaborative relationship entails one that is highly positive and supportive of staff, such as promoting professional development opportunities, acknowledging staff members, and respecting all staff members. As discussed in Chapter 5, this also entails:

- Guaranteeing systems of communications and input that encompass all district stakeholders (internal and external) and monitoring the level of trust between the district and its schools
- Ensuring collaborative goal setting (formulation of district ends: mission, vision, values, and district goals) to help promote *equity* for all students
- Ensuring systems for capacity building (e.g., professional development)

Indicator B — District and School Level Teams

The district and school level teams collaborate to collect, analyze, and apply student learning data continuously from a variety of sources, including comparison and trend data about student learning, instruction, program evaluation, organizational conditions, and fiscal resources that support student learning.

PLO Alignment

The ALT works directly with TLTs to collect, analyze, and form conclusions about student data as well as the following:

- Assist staff in forming conclusions concerning student data (e.g., limitations to the data; what the data doesn't tell us)
- Establish systems in order for staff to measure student academic performance periodically (e.g., trend data, program evaluation, organizational conditions)
- Ensure student data is easily assessable for staff members and is easy to analyze and to apply
- Ensure student data is used to make informed decisions concerning student progress
- Support staff in meeting districtwide goals including how resources will be distributed (e.g., ensuring common staff plan times and professional development opportunities)

Indicator C — Teacher Leadership

The teachers actively model and foster a positive school environment in which educators and students feel valued and are challenged to be engaged and to grow.

PLO Alignment

- The BLT meets periodically to ensure that school staff promotes highly positive classroom environments, demonstrates respect for all students, and challenges all students to achieve high expectations. Further, the BLT ensures alignment between district and school objectives.
- TLTs meet regularly to discuss grade and/or departmental expectations that students are to meet based on common formative and summative assessments, which are grounded on high expectations.

Indicator D — Student Leadership

The students actively participate in leadership opportunities that develop self-direction and a sense of responsibility for improving self, school, and community.

PLO Alignment

- PLOs seek input from all stakeholders concerning the direction of the district. The GLT expects the ALT to provide student input when establishing district ends such as through surveys and focus groups.
- BLTs and TLTs provide opportunities for student leadership (student groups and clubs) and promote the use of cooperative learning among all students.

Standard IV — Governance, Management, and Operations

In successful districts and schools, efficient and effective governance policies and administrative procedures assure that personnel, fiscal resources, and data/technology systems promote and support student performance and school effectiveness.

Indicator A — Personnel

The district has school board policies and administrative procedures that provide for a comprehensive approach to recurring, evaluating, and sustaining highly qualified personnel.

PLO Alignment

The school board provides authority to its superintendent by relying on board policies. These policies address and codify school board operations and key district ends (e.g., hiring and sustaining a highly qualified workforce, recruitment and mentoring, and professional development). Board policies cannot be used only to delegate authority to the superintendent but can also be used to provide perimeters to that authority in addition to how board policies will be monitored. Note: It is the job of the superintendent to ensure that administrative procedures (operations) are properly aligned with board policies.

Additionally, board policies do the following:

- Allow the board to become more familiar with its policies and that policies are up to date
- Ensure that board initiatives are being met
- Ensure the legal operation of the district
- Provide a formal means for board accountability
- Build trust among stakeholders

Indicator B—Fiscal Resources

The school board and the superintendent work collaboratively to identify and allocate/reallocate resources needed for effective implementation of a comprehensive system of continuous improvement.

PLO Alignment

- The GLT not only works collaboratively to determine district ends but also works collaboratively to identify resources to support district goals. Note: The superintendent presents to the board a strategic plan of how to meet district goals based on multiple data sources, which the board approves or disapproves.
- The GLT ensures that the strategic plan and action plan are made available to stakeholders concerning not only the direction of the district but also how the district plans to bring district ends into reality.

Indicator C—Data Collection and Technology Tools

The school board and superintendent work collaboratively to monitor and evaluate the implementation of the continuous improvement process through an ongoing data collection system supported by an effective technology infrastructure.

PLO Alignment

- In PLO organizations, the board and superintendent designate meeting times specifically to discuss overall district ends and to monitor the implementation of district ends including any modifications that may be needed.
- School boards in PLO organizations are not solely dependent on the superintendent for information regarding district ends but instead receive verbal

and written reports from a myriad of district stakeholders regarding district ends.

- The ALT works collaboratively to determine technological needs and how technology may be used to support district and/or school continuous improvement efforts.

Standard V — Educator and Employee Quality

In successful districts and schools, all personnel participate in processes of self-reflection, collaboration, and evaluation that lead to professional growth and development in order to create and maintain a high-quality learning community.

Indicator A — Professional Development

All educators engage in continuous learning opportunities for professional growth designed to improve school and classroom practice as defined by the academic, physical, social, emotional, and behavioral programming needs.

PLO Alignment

- In PLO organizations, a myriad of stakeholders assist in the development of district ends. District ends are utilized as the basis of the superintendent's evaluation and are necessary to provide direction to the superintendent. The superintendent ensures that principals and other administrators are working toward district ends, principals ensure that the work of teachers and other staff members aligns with district objectives, and teachers ensure students are aware of district expectations.
- Staff professional development is primarily aligned to district ends. The ALT ensures that professional development opportunities are provided to staff so that district goals and objectives are being implemented with fidelity.
- In a PLO, the GLT ensures that it has delegated proper authority to the superintendent for district ends to be carried out.
- TLTs meet to discuss the need for professional development in regard to improving teacher classroom instructional practices, which are data driven and based on students' academic, physical, social, emotional, and behavioral needs.
- TLTs/BLTs allow for teachers to meet and to share professional development resources.
- TLTs/BLTs seek to ensure that professional development opportunities are systematically monitored.

Indicator B—Professional Collaboration

All educators collaborate on the improvement of the learning environment through the study of relevant data, problem analysis, and the implementation of strategies that improve delivery of services in all schools of the district.

PLO Alignment

- The nature of the PLO is based on the premise that systemic collaboration is the key to continuous, sustained student achievement and helps promote equitable outcomes for all students. Chapter 5 details the roles and responsibilities of various PLC teams and how they all work collaboratively to improve student achievement, beginning with the establishment of district ends.
- The ALT ensures that TLTs have access to relevant data including how to properly interpret data.
- The ALT assists TLTs to help identify strategies that may be used to help improve the delivery of services based on relevant data.

Indicator C—Support Personnel Professional Development

All support personnel engage in continuous learning opportunities for professional growth designed to improve professional performance.

PLO Alignment

- In a PLO, it is common for support staff to have a support staff learning team and a member of the team to be represented on the school's BLT. (Note: It is the job of the ALT to help determine the number and focus of district learning teams based on district needs.)
- Similar to TLTs, the ALT works with the support staff learning team to identify and encourage professional development opportunities.
- Professional development should be aligned to district ends as well as to improve student academic, physical, social, emotional, and behavioral needs.

Indicator D—Evaluation, Feedback, and Support

All personnel participate in a comprehensive evaluation process that utilizes multiple interactive communication tools to facilitate self-reflection and to inform the process of professional growth.

PLO Alignment

- In a PLO, it is the job of the ALT to ensure that all licensed personnel collaborate with administrators for the purpose of conducting staff evaluations aimed at improving student achievement and classroom instructional strategies.
- Administrators see to it that staff is given frequent and targeted feedback.
- In a PLO, the collaborative culture produces a culture based on trust. Trust is needed in order for staff not to feel that evaluations will be used as a "gotcha."
- Themes that emerge in the evaluation processes may be addressed in different venues including in TLT meetings.

Standard VI—Family and Community Engagement

In successful districts and schools, stakeholders have significant opportunities to develop, implement, and plan parent-involvement practices and compacts to have ongoing communication regarding student physical, social, emotional, behavioral, and academic growth.

Indicator A—School-to-Home Connections

District/school personnel and primary caregivers engage in regular communication to provide mutual supports and guidance between home and school for all aspects of student learning.

PLO Alignment

- In a PLO, family and community engagement is vital to the success of the district, and their opinions are strongly valued.
- The GLT ensures that family and community stakeholders are represented during the formulation of district ends.
- The ALT ensures that district schools have a plan in place for engaging family and community stakeholders.

  - The BLT facilitates and monitors the family and community engagement process including ensuring that TLTs utilize various strategies for engaging family and community stakeholders (e.g., phone logs, guest speakers, parent conferences) and taking into consideration diverse school populations.

Indicator B—Student Personal Development

The district and school leverage existing resources to provide a coordinated system of support for the whole child.

PLO Alignment

- The BLT discusses various resources available to assist in the development of the whole child, and this information is then shared with the TLTs.
- The BLTs/TLTs share relevant information with family and community stakeholders concerning things they can do to support the well-being of students.

Indicator C—Student Advocates

Educators communicate regularly with primary caregivers and various community agencies and encourage them to participate as active partners in the development of the whole child.

PLO Alignment

- The ALT shares information with principals regarding various community resources and how partnering with various agencies may benefit students. This information is shared with the BLTs and also shared with the TLTs. Note: The governance team approves all district community partnerships.
- The BLT ensures that caregivers have opportunities to serve as partners in the educational process including serving on parent advisory groups.
- The BLT works with TLTs to ensure that TLTs discuss various ways in which caregivers can be given opportunities to participate in the educational process.

Standard VII—Student and Learning Development

In successful districts and schools, curriculum, instruction, and assessment are monitored and adjusted systematically in response to data from multiple assessments of student learning, an examination of professional practice, and analysis of learning conditions to improve student growth continuously.

Indicator A—Instructional Planning and Preparation

Instructional staff and district/school leadership ensure that instructional planning is based on the district's curriculum as aligned with established learning standards and as supported by appropriate resources and professional development.

PLO Alignment

- In a PLO, TLTs are engaged in various operations to ensure that students have a viable and guaranteed curriculum based on the district's curriculum.
- TLTs unpack learning standards (e.g., curriculum maps) and create common formative and summative assessments to gauge student learning.
- ALTs work to ensure that TLTs are aware of the district's curriculum and objectives as well as state learning standards. Also, ALTs work to ensure that TLTs have the necessary resources to deliver the curriculum with fidelity.
- ALTs ensure that TLTs are given time to meet to discuss curriculum and student achievement measures.

Indicator B — Classroom Management

Instructional staff and district/school leadership collaborate to provide an instructional environment that actively engages all students by using effective, varied, and research-based practices to meet the academic and social/emotional needs of the whole child and empower students to share responsibility for their learning.

PLO Alignment

- A key foundation of the PLO is the level of collaboration among all district stakeholders but especially between the ALTs and TLTs to ensure that the instructional learning environment is based on researched-based practices or, in other words, ensure that instruction is results oriented.
- ALTs (which include the principal) utilize the BLT as a conduit to ensure that TLTs are addressing the social/emotional learning needs of students as well as ensuring a "response to intervention" for struggling learners.
- TLTs seek to ensure that personalized learning occurs and motivates students to take ownership of their learning.

Indicator C — Delivery of Instruction

Instructional staff, supported by district/school leadership, utilizes instruction, evaluation, and assessment strategies that are informed by research to monitor instruction continuously, adjusting to the needs of the whole child.

PLO Alignment

- ALTs and BLTs ensure that instructional staff are given time to collaborate and to make available resources that enable educators to utilize research-based strategies for instruction, evaluation, and assessment.
- ALTs and BLTs ensure that educators utilize a myriad of data when assessing student learning and making any necessary adjustments to meet the needs of the whole child.
- Note: The GLT approves a budget and resources to meet district ends based on the recommendation of the superintendent. This includes providing the necessary resources to staff.

Indicator D—Professional Responsibilities

Instructional staff and district/school leadership collaboratively monitor the teacher evaluation system to ensure consistent implementation that supports the work of the school/district to improve teaching and learning.

PLO Alignment

- The ALT and BLT help to ensure that the teacher evaluation system is implemented with fidelity and with consistent implementation.
- The ALT and BLT monitor the teacher evaluation system to ensure improvements in the delivery of instruction and learning and student performance.
- The ALT and BLT provide relevant professional development opportunities to address staff deficiencies.

   The proof is overwhelming that PLOs are beneficial because of their unique flexibilities in meeting the unique needs and ends (e.g., mission, vision, goals) of local school districts and simultaneously promoting student achievement. More importantly, PLOs undeniably promote *equity* for all district students by allowing for various stakeholders to have a voice concerning what equity looks like for their district based on demographics and available resources.
   The former state superintendent of Montana, Denise Juneau, believes that in order ultimately to improve student achievement, direction must come from the local level with input from various stakeholders. Juneau (2018) affirmed her belief in collaborative governance when she noted, "When I was the state superintendent in Montana, I understood that meaningful change has to be decided at the local level and supported by those at the top. There is no better approach than to work side-by-side with school staff, community

members, and students to change their educational system, let them define their future, and then support their efforts to reach their goals."

As noted in this chapter, PLOs can adapt to rural, urban, and suburban districts regardless of district size and can be adjusted to meet state and federal standards. PLOs can serve as a catalyst for promoting systemic improvement, promoting greater transparency, fostering increased stakeholder (internal and external) support, and enhancing school board and superintendent relations. DuFour and Eaker (1998) emphasized that "the most promising strategy for sustained, substantive school improvement is developing the ability of school personnel to function as professional learning communities."

School boards and their superintendents must create a sense of urgency if they truly hope to transform school districts. Although it takes time and patience to put the right systems in place to improve organizational effectiveness and district culture, once in place governance teams will discover that the district can run on "cruise control," if the right systems, including monitoring systems, are in place. These systems entail identifying and monitoring priorities (based on stakeholder input), detecting the conditions they expect to see in every district school, building staff capacity to meet district expectations, investing in collaborative systems, and continuing to assess the district's climate in an effort to improve district culture.

The bottom line is that school boards must make a decision to transform district culture from the boardroom to the classroom without relying on canned educational programs. School boards must bear in mind that their leadership impacts the district's culture because their leadership will impact staff behavior, which will, in turn, affect the organization's results.

PLOs allow governance teams with an opportunity to provide effective leadership which is vital to enhancing the organization's effectiveness. As George Couros (2015), author of *The Innovator's Mindset*, stated, "The ability to innovate—to create something new and better—is a skill that organizations worldwide are looking for." PLOs allow school districts opportunities to be innovative and truly transformational in ensuring that all students learn at high levels.

Chapter Ten

Concluding Thoughts

A PLO is a professional learning organization led by the governance team (school board and superintendent) for the purpose of ensuring systemic collaboration and communication within an entire school district. PLOs are guided by the key belief that all district staff members should have the ability to collaborate and communicate with peers toward the success of district ends (e.g., core values/beliefs, mission, vision, and goals). Everyone in the district is learning in a 360-degree scope from the boardroom to the classroom.

This dynamic new term (PLO) sets a new paradigm in the educational culture. It invites the governance team to be an integral part of learning more about the school district and its schools more effectively. More importantly, a PLO empowers the board to truly transform the district's culture.

School boards perform and govern differently from district to district. Some school boards are disengaged while others are too engaged. Disengaged boards overly rely on the superintendent to handle all the operations of the school district without any kind of guidance regarding expectations and/or the monitoring of expectations. On the other hand, there are school boards that attempt to micromanage all the operational aspects of the district. Dr. Rice's model supports my belief that school boards are less likely to engage in micromanagement if they properly understand what is occurring throughout as it relates to district ends.

Finally, there are boards that fall into various spectrums between uninformed delegation and micromanagement, and/or practice, or what Alsbury and Gore (2015) referred to as balanced governance, for which a PLO advocates.

Dr. Rice is to be commended for establishing a PLO model that allows school boards to be properly informed about what is occurring throughout the district as it relates to district ends. His model also allows boards to stay informed about how systemic collaboration and communication take place between all internal and external stakeholders to carry out successfully the mission of the organization.

Collaborative structures keep the board informed as to whether they are on the right track as elected trustees of the district and to assist the board in gaining buy-in regarding district priorities. Since leadership starts from the top, a PLO sends the message that the school board is also engaged in learning, thus rounding out the entire PLO.

School boards are opening their eyes and minds to the concept that governance teams need to understand the benefits of a collaborative governance style that encompasses a variety of district stakeholders. Traditionally, a school board was composed of community members who received all their information from the superintendent. Modern-day beliefs, however, are that board members and the superintendent should not only work more collaboratively toward district ends but should also value stakeholder input when making educational decisions. No longer can the governance team be a polarizing entity, but it can become a unifying entity, inclusive of all stakeholders involved.

PLO organizations significantly increase student achievement. PLOs bridge all the connected parts or stakeholders of the district in order for the school system to ensure that all students learn at high levels and are given what they need in order to be successful. Therefore, PLOs are rooted in *equity* for all students. PLOs ensure that all stakeholders have a voice in the direction of the district that impacts student outcomes. Professional learning communities (PLCs) are created to serve as the bridge connecting all the various parts and roles (strategic, tactical, and operational) of the district. Simply, PLCs are the subcommittees, learning teams of the district that compose the PLO.

Collaboration is desperately needed to form the culture of true teamwork within a school district. The community will be more cohesive, understanding, trusting, and productive if all stakeholders collaboratively work toward the end in mind and clearly have buy-in about what the goals and outcomes should be. In addition, collaboration between governance teams and teachers will minimize the "us-versus-them" mentality that often exists between those groups. Essentially, board members and teachers will be motivated to operate as a team because of the internal pressures to work together that a collaborative culture yields.

The author explains what the organizational culture should encompass. A district's culture should be unique and should represent the values of the community it serves. The culture is not confined to a particular building or school, but it does represent the attitude of the entire organization. The organizational culture refers to the quality and character of the organization based upon various stakeholders' views of the organization. Stakeholder buy-in is a key component to the culture of a collaborative governance model.

The author also explains how PLOs can best assist the school board with its number one task of clarifying the district's purpose by defining and articulating district ends. Effective school boards ensure that the district's vision and goals are galvanized with two ends in mind—student learning and organizational effectiveness. This includes input from the internal and external public. To successfully clarify the district's purpose and in order for a district to successfully transform into a PLO organization, the board and superintendent must be a good fit. This entails agreeing on a common direction and sharing the same belief in the philosophy of collaborative governance.

Most educators simply view a professional learning community or PLC as a group of educators or staff who meet regularly, share expertise, and work collaboratively to improve teaching skills and the academic performance of students. This new concept of a PLO encompasses the board and other key stakeholders in order to have systemic alignment and an organizational system built on collaboration and on communication. As Dr. Rice describes, PLOs would now include the following components of the PLCs: (1) the principals, (2) teachers/staff, and (3) students/parents/community, as well as the governance team—board members and the superintendent.

Dr. Rice's PLO model transforms the dynamics of a district completely to a new concept. The school board can govern more effectively by practicing the concept of informed oversight embedded in the PLO model rather than always receiving reports from one person—the superintendent—concerning district operations. Facilitated by the superintendent, various district PLC teams will now be able to inform the school board of the implementation of district ends. Again, the governance team will now feel empowered, and better informed, by staff members through an approved communication link endorsed by the superintendent and school board.

School boards should reflect on student learning in every decision they make and know the results they expect the district to attain. The strategic plan is the glue that links the PLO system together based on collective common interests and goals. Incorporating the three main ideas of a PLO (e.g., focus on learning, focus on results, and focus on collaboration) will support the board in its vision that drives governance team decision-making regarding student learning, deciding what the results should be, and what monitoring data may be needed. The monitoring of data should include the triangulation of data that will help the governance team determine if ends or outcomes have been met.

There are numerous benefits for districts that choose to become PLOs, including collaborative buy-in, collaborative participation, decision-making, joint communication, team building, systemic collaborative relationships and approaches, systemic school improvement, systemwide framework, entities interconnected, professional development, informed decisions, balanced governance approach, increased motivation and meaning in pushing toward agreed-upon ends, enhanced organizational effectiveness, creativity, enriched community engagement efforts, improved collective bargaining process, greater transparency, and much more.

All stakeholders benefit in many ways, according to their involvement and desire to increase student achievement in a PLO. Dr. Rice's book provides new insight into how systemic collaboration among the internal/external stakeholders in a school district can be monumental in the success of children.

This new educational concept brings about systemic districtwide collaboration and communication among all parties within a school district. Dr. Rice's approach strays from the past practice of those educational pundits who have classified PLCs as something solely for teachers. I am convinced that Dr. Rice's educational model will forever change the landscape and the culture of education, and this promising educational innovation is called PLO!

Dr. Pam Manning
Former Superintendent and Professor, McKendree University

Glossary

Balanced governance is a "school governance approach that supports and promotes 'balance'—discouraging micromanaging on one end of the governance continuum and a disengaged, rubber-stamping board on the other" (Alsbury & Gore, 2015).

Civic capacity refers to the "ability of business leaders, union leaders, civic leaders, educational leaders, and leaders of other significant organizations to work together on behalf of common goals. Developing such civic capacity builds trust, a common identity, and the willingness to work with shared purpose for the success of the school or schools within the system" (Carbaugh et al., 2015).

Collaborative leadership is about "capitalizing on the strengths and skills of others in the effort to achieve common goals . . . collaborative leadership is about encouraging others to be leaders as well" (Martin & Rains, 2018). Collaborative leadership entails bringing the appropriate people together in constructive ways with good information, thus creating authentic visions and strategies for addressing the shared concerns of the organization or community.

Collaborative governance is "a governing arrangement in which one or more public agencies directly engage non-state stakeholders in a collective decision-making process that is formal, consensus-oriented, and deliberative and that aims to make or implement public policy or manage public programs or assets" (Ansell & Gash, 2007).

Consciously uninformed is a term used to describe what a person, group, and or organization is not fully aware of; however, need more information to properly understand it (N. Osborne, personal communication, March 5, 2018).

Cooperative learning is an educational approach based on active student engagement that entails students working in groups to complete tasks collectively toward academic goals (Johnson, Johnson, & Stanne, 2000).

District ends are the values and beliefs, mission, vision, and goals that clarify the district's purpose or reason for existing (IASB, 2017).

Equity for students entails ensuring that each student has what he or she needs to be successful. Equity has many handles such as racial, technology, and funding. School districts must ensure that their systems, policies, and practices are equitable for all students.

Focus on collaboration entails how systemic collaboration and communication are fostered throughout the district to ensure organizational effectiveness (Carbaugh et al., 2015).

Focus on learning entails what students should know and be able to do and includes what assistance will be provided to students who have learning difficulties (DuFour & Eaker, 1998).

Focus on results encompasses how district expectations (district goals) are being monitored and includes access to meaningful data, as well as how issues are resolved, and how the district celebrates its success (DuFour & Eaker, 1998).

Informed oversight is the name given to school boards, especially those in PLO districts that have a thorough understanding of how the district operates, and boards that verify the information they receive to ensure its accuracy.

Informed oversight enables the board to understand better the means or process/procedures required to reach district ends (e.g., mission, vision, goals) of the district (Alsbury & Gore, 2015). The concept of "trust but verify" is essential to the governing concept of "informed oversight." "Trust but verify" entails how the board can validate information by relying on various verification processes.

Operational role (e.g., TLT) implements tactical plans that allow the organization to meet strategic goals. Operationalists field-test tactical plans and are generally composed of teachers, instructional coaches, and various other staff members (Van Clay et al., 2011).

Organizational culture refers to the quality and character of the organization based upon various stakeholders' views of the organization. Elements of organizational culture in a school district include safety, relationships, and the condition of the teaching and learning environment. According to Psychology and Society (n.d.), organizational culture reflects the values, beliefs, and norms that characterize an organization as a whole.

Professional learning communities (PLCs) are collaborative departmentalized learning teams established by PLOs as a vehicle to be used to accomplish the work of the organization. Internal (stakeholders that work in the district) learning teams are arranged by strategic, tactical, and operational roles.

Attributes of PLCs are supportive and shared leadership, collective creativity, shared values, and vision developed from an unswerving commitment to student learning. The key concepts of a PLC are also those of the PLO, which are the following: a focus on learning, a focus on results, and a focus on collaboration (Carbaugh et al.,2015; Hord, 1997).

Common PLC teams are governance, administrative, building, teachers, parents, students, and district learning teams. Note: Teacher teams are most commonly referred to as a PLC because PLOs began with teachers.

Professional learning organization (PLO) is a name given to reflect the entire collaborative district. PLCs are used to departmentalize the organization into manageable systems based on the division of human labor and their role and responsibility regarding the work to be completed. The strategic (school board plus superintendent), tactical (administration), and operational (staff) roles are the three essential professional learning communities and/or learning teams or departments that formulate the PLO.

A PLO entails supportive and shared leadership, supportive conditions for collective inquiry and learning, and common values and beliefs about improving student learning. The key concepts of a PLO are the following: a focus on learning, a focus on results, and a focus on collaboration. A PLO lends legitimacy to the learning communities under its larger umbrella.

PLOs create and maintain networks of learning communities and use these networks as the primary means by which the work of the organization is accomplished (Schlechty, 2009).

Role bridger refers to someone who can serve as a bridge between two or more other district roles such as strategic, tactical, or operational (Van Clay et al., 2011).

Site-based management calls for greater building-level decision-making in areas such as instruction, personnel, budget, and policy. This redistribution of power is based on the concept of decentralized control (Alsbury & Gore, 2015).

Strategic role (GLT) is responsible for clarifying the district's purpose or articulating the big picture or ends (e.g., mission, vision, values, goals) for the school district and is committed to monitoring. The strategic role is customer focused. The strategists consist of the school board in partnership with the superintendent (Van Clay et al., 2011).

Tactical role (ALT) is responsible for drafting plans to implement successfully the strategic goals set by the governance team or school board. Tacticians are generally composed of the superintendent and various school district administrators (Van Clay et al., 2011).

Triangulation of data uses multiple data sources to produce common themes as well as to verify information (Qualitative Research Guidelines Project, n.d.).

References

Abulon, E., & Saquilabon, J. (2016). Enhancing academic performance through parental involvement strategies. *The Normal Lights—Journal on Teacher Education.* Retrieved from http://po.pnuresearchportal.org/ejournal/index.php/normallights/article/view/274.

Alsbury, T., & Gore, P. (2015). *Improving school board effectiveness: A balanced governance approach.* Cambridge, MA: Harvard Education Press.

Ansell, C., & Gash, C. (2007). Collaborative governance in theory and practice. *Journal of Public Administration Research and Theory,* 543–571.

Balch, B., & Adamson, M. (2017). *Building great school board–superintendent teams.* Bloomington, IN: Solution Tree Press.

Bartz, D., Collins-Ayanlaja, C., & Rice, P. (2017). African-American parents and effective parent involvement programs. *Schooling, 8*(1). Retrieved from http://www.nationalforum.com/Electronic%20Journal%20Volumes/Bartz,%20David%20African-American%20Parents%20an%20Effective%20Parent%20Involvement%20Programs%20SCHOOLING%20V8%20N1%202017.pdf.

Bartz, D., Rice, P., & Karnes, C. (2018a, March). Building a collaborative relationship between the school board and superintendent. Illinois Association of School Administrators, *Leadership Matters,* 18–19.

Bartz, D., Rice, P., & Karnes, C. (2018b). Community engagement: A key ingredient for public schools gaining stakeholders' input and support. *National Forum of Educational Administration and Supervision Journal, 36*(4), 1–7.

Bartz, D., Thompson, K., & Rice, P. (2017). Maximizing the human capital of millennials through supervisors using performance management. *International Journal of Management, Business, and Administration, 20*(1).

Bimber, B. A. (1993). *School decentralization: Lessons from the study of bureaucracy.* Santa Monica, CA: Rand, 1993.

Boyle, P., & Burns, D. (2011). *Preserving the public in public schools.* Lanham, MD: Rowman & Littlefield.

Carbaugh, B., Marzano, R., & Toth, M. (2015). *School leadership for results: Shifting the focus of leader evaluation.* West Palm Beach, FL: Learning Sciences International.

Carroll, T., & Doerr, H. (2010). Learning teams and the future of teaching. *Education Week, 37*(28). Retrieved from https://www.edweek.org/ew/articles/2010/06/28/36carroll.h29.html.

Carver, J. (2001). *John Carver on board leadership.* San Francisco, CA. Jossey-Bass.

Center for Public Education (n.d.). Eight characteristics of effective school boards. Retrieved from http://www.centerforpubliceducation.org/research/eight-characteristics-effective-school-boards-full-report.

Chrislip, D., & Larson, C. (1994). *Collaborative leadership: How citizens and civic leaders can make a difference*. San Francisco, CA: Jossey-Bass.

Chubb, J. E., & Moe, T. M. (1990). *Politics, markets and America's schools*. Washington, DC: The Brookings Institution.

Clark, B. (2017, November–December). Combining strategic planning, community engagement. *Illinois School Board Journal, 85*(6), 2–4.

Collins, J. (2001). *Good to Great*. New York, NY: HarperCollins.

Couros, G. (2015). *The Innovator's Mindset*. San Diego, CA: Dave Burgess Consulting.

Cunningham, N. (2016). *Elementary district-level and building-level leadership practices that promote and sustain professional learning communities* (Doctoral dissertation, Illinois State University).

Desloge, B. (2017). In search of civility. NACo. Retrieved from http://www.naco.org/resources/civility.

DuFour, R., DuFour, R. B., & Eaker, R. E. (2008). *Revisiting professional learning communities at work: New insights for improving schools*. Bloomington, IN: Solution Tree Press.

DuFour, R., DuFour, R. B., Eaker, R. E., & Many, T. (2006). *Learning by doing: A handbook for professional learning communities at work*. Bloomington, IN: Solution Tree Press.

DuFour, R., & Eaker, R. E. (1998). *Professional learning communities at work: Best practices for enhancing student achievement*. Bloomington, IN: National Education Service.

Duhigg, C. (2016). What Google learned from its quest to build the perfect team. *New York Times*. Retrieved from https://www.nytimes.com/2016/02/28/magazine/what-google-learned-from-its-quest-to-build-the-perfect-team.html.

Eggert, D., & Williams, C. (2017). Plan to shut Detroit's failing schools reveals lack of options. *Education Week, 36*(25), 9.

Enna. (2013). How kaizen improves the three key drivers of employee engagement. Retrieved from https://enna.com/2013/01/10/how-kaizen-improves-the-three-key-drivers-of-employee-engagement/.

Friend, M., & Cook, L. (2013). *Interactions: Collaboration skills for school professionals*. Boston, MA: Pearson.

Gewertz, C. (2017). The hard work of making school for everybody. *Education Week, 36*(25), pp. 1, 12.

Green, M. (2017). Kirsten Gillibrand drops F-bomb during speech on democracy. CNN. Retrieved from https://www.cnn.com/2017/06/09/politics/kirsten-gillibrand-fbomb/index.html.

Gregory, G. (n.d.). Why all-star teams fail: Strategies to get everyone to play together. Retrieved from http://www.reliableplant.com/Read/11603/why-all-star-teams-fail-strategies-to-get-everyone-to-play-toger.

Gruenert, S. (2008, March/April). School culture/school climate: They are not the same thing. *Principal*. Retrieved from https://www.naesp.org/sites/default/files/resources/2/Principal/2008/M-Ap56.pdf.

Honawar, V. (2008). Working smarter by working together. *Education Week*. Retrieved from https://www.edweek.org/ew/articles/2008/04/02/31plc_ep.h27.html.

Hord, S. M. (1997). *Professional learning communities: Communities of continuous inquiry and improvement*. Austin, TX: Southwest Educational Development Laboratory.

Illinois Association of School Boards. (2000). IASB'S Lighthouse study: School boards and student achievement. *Iowa School Board Compass, 5*(2), 1–12.

Illinois Association of School Boards. (2017). Foundational principles of effective governance. Retrieved from https://www.iasb.com/principles.cfm.

Illinois Association of School Boards. (2018). Connecting with the community. Retrieved from http://iasb.mys1cloud.com/communityengagement.pdf.

Illinois School Board News Blog. (2018). Effingham shares model for empowering teachers. Retrieved from http://blog.iasb.com/2018/04/effingham-shares-model-for-empowering.html.

Illinois State Board of Education. (n.d.). *The Illinois State Board of Education Quality Framework for Illinois School Districts*. Retrieved from https://www.isbe.net/Documents/quality-framework-160505.pdf.

James, T. J. (1982). Educational administration and organization: A 40-year perspective. *Educational Researcher, 11*(2), 14–18.

Johnson, D., Johnson, R., & Stanne, M. (2000). Cooperative learning methods: A meta-analysis. *University of Minnesota*. Retrieved from https://www.lcps.org/cms/lib4/VA01000195/Centricity/Domain/124/Cooperative%20Learning%20Methods%20A%20Meta-Analysis.pdf.

Juneau, D. (2018). The Bureau of Indian Education is broken. *Education Week, 37*(19), 32.

Klein, A. (2013). After early progress, Ky. school struggles to turn around. *Education Week, 37*(29). Retrieved from https://www.edweek.org/ew/articles/2013/06/12/35shawnee_ep.h32.html.

Kracke, N. (2006, April). Public engagement. *NSPRA's Network Newsletter*. Retrieved from https://www.nspra.org/public_engagement.

Leithwood, K., Seashore Louis, K., Anderson, S., & Wahlstrom, K. (2004). *How leadership influences student learning*. Retrieved from http://www.wallacefoundation.org/Knowledge-Center/KnowledgeTopics/CurrentAreasofFocus/ EducationLeadership/Pages/HowLeadershipInfluencesStudentLearning.aspx.

Maehr, M. L., Hartman, A., & Bartz, D. E. (1984). Mandatory metropolitan solutions to desegregation problems: The social psychological harm of an administrative remedy. In D. E. Bartz and M. L. Maehr (Eds.), *Advances in motivation and achievement* (pp. 301–316). Greenwich, CT: JAI Press.

Martin, K. (n.d.). Using kaizen for employee engagement and improvement. QAspire.com. Retrieved from http://qaspire.com/2013/02/15/using-kaizen-for-employee-engagement-and-improvement/.

Martin, T., & Rains, C. (2018). *Stronger together: Answering the questions of collaborative leadership*. Bloomington, IN: Solution Tree Press.

Marzano, R. (2003). *What works in schools: Translating research into action*. Alexandria, VA: Association for Supervision and Curriculum Development.

Marzano, R., Pickering, D., & Pollock, J. (2001). *Classroom instruction that works*. Alexandria, VA: Association for Supervision & Curriculum Development.

Marzano, R., & Waters, T. (2009). *District leadership that works: Striking the right balance*. Bloomington, IN: Solution Tree Press.

Maxwell, J. (2001). *The 17 indisputable laws of teamwork: Embrace them and empower your team*. Nashville, TN: Thomas Nelson.

Maxwell, L. (2014). U.S. school enrollment hits majority–minority milestone. *Education Week*. Retrieved from https://www.edweek.org/ew/articles/2014/08/20/01demographics.h34.html.

Merica, D. (2017). Sh-t Talking is Democrats' new strategy. CNN. Retrieved from www.cnn.com/2017/04/24/politics/tom-perez-swearing-trump/index.html.

MetLife. (2009). *The MetLife survey of the American teacher: Collaborating for student success.*. Retrieved from https://eric.ed.gov/?id=ED509650.

Metzger, A. (2016). Union officials and elected Democrats rally against MBTA privatization. *State House News Service*. Retrieved from http://www.wbur.org/news/2016/10/12/rally-against-mbta-privatization.

MindTools. (n.d.). Kaizen: Gaining the full benefits of continuous improvement. Retrieved from https://www.mindtools.com/pages/article/newSTR_97.htm.

National Center for Educational Statistics. (n.d.). Schools and staffing survey. Retrieved from https://nces.ed.gov/surveys/sass/.

National Council on Teacher Quality (2017). Time spent on teacher collaboration. *Education Week, 37*(15), 5.

Osborne, N. Personal communication, March 5, 2018.

Process Improvement Japan. (n.d.). *Motivation in the workplace*. Retrieved from http://www.process-improvement-japan.com/motivation-in-the-workplace.html.

Psychology and Society (n.d.). *Organizational culture*. Retrieved from http://www.psychologyandsociety.com/organizationalculture.html.

Qualitative Research Guidelines Project (n.d.). Triangulation. *Robert Wood Johnson Foundation*. Retrieved from http://www.qualres.org/HomeTria-3692.html.

Rice, P. (2014). *Vanishing school boards: Where school boards have gone, why we need them, and how we can bring them back.* Lanham, MD: Rowman & Littlefield.

Sawchuk, S. (2014). NEA aims to revive organizing as membership drops. *Education Week.* Retrieved from https://www.edweek.org/ew/articles/2014/06/04/33organize_ep.h33.html.

Schlechty, P. (2009). *Leading for learning: How to transform schools into learning organizations.* San Francisco, CA: Jossey-Bass.

Senge, P. (2006). *The fifth discipline: The art and practice of the learning organization.* New York, NY: Currency Doubleday.

Smith, M. (2012). *Why leadership sucks.* Retrieved from http://www.milesanthonysmith.com/uploads/1/4/0/0/14006904/why_leadership_sucks_preview_shorter.pdf.

Sparks, S. (2017). Classroom collaboration: Seeking the secret to success. *Education Week, 36*(31), 8.

Sparks, S. (2018a). A look at how principals really drive school improvement. *Education Week.* Retrieved from http://blogs.edweek.org/edweek/inside-school-research/2018/03/how_principals_drive_student_improvement.html?cmp=eml-enl-eu-mostpop&M=58478397&U=1075899.

Sparks, S. (2018b). Tinkering toward a better education system. *Education Week, 37*(19), pp. 1, 14.

Superville, D. (2017). Boards pay big bucks to make supes leave. *Education Week, 36*(31), pp. 1, 16.

Sutter, J. (2017). The kids Suing Donald Trump are marching to the White House. CNN. Retrieved from https://www.cnn.com/2017/04/29/politics/sutter-climate-kids-march-washington/index.html.

Togneri, W., & Anderson, S. (2003). How high poverty districts improve. *Leadership, 33*(1), 12–16.

Turow, S. (2011). Let-them-eat-cake-attitude threatens to destroy a network of public assets. *Huffington Post.* Retrieved from https://www.huffingtonpost.com/scott-turow/letthemeatcakeattitude-th_b_823609.html.

Tyack, D. (1974). *The one best system: A history of American urban education.* Cambridge, MA: Harvard University Press.

Tyack, D. (2002). Forgotten players: How local school districts shaped American education. In A. M. Hightower, M. S. Knapp, J. A. Marsh, and M. W. McLaughlin (Eds.), *School districts and instructional renewal* (pp. 9–24). New York, NY: Teachers College Press.

Tzu, S. (1994). *The art of war* (R. Sawyer, Trans.). Boulder, CO: Westview Press.

U.S. Department of Education (n.d.). *Every Student Succeeds Act (ESSA).* U.S. Department of Education. Retrieved from https://www.ed.gov/ESSA.

Van Clay, M., & Soldwedel, P. (2009). *The school board fieldbook: Leading with vision.* Bloomington, IN: Solution Tree Press.

Van Clay, M., Soldwedel, P., & Many, T. (2011). *Aligning school districts as PLCs.* Bloomington, IN: Solution Tree Press.

Vocoli. (2014). When GM adopted Toyota's secret sauce with kaizen. Retrieved from https://www.vocoli.com/blog/december-2014/when-gm-adopted-toyota-s-secret-sauce/.

Will, M. (2016). Florida teachers push back on mandated collaboration. *Education Week, 36*(2), 4.

Will, M. (2017a). Study: When teachers have a say in schools, students score higher. *Education Week, 37*(11), 8.

Will, M. (2017b). Teacher job satisfaction and student achievement. *Education Week, 36*(23), 5.

About the Author

Dr. **Patrick Rice** is the field services/equity director for the Illinois Association of School Boards. From 2006 to 2010, he was an adjunct professor for McKendree College in Lebanon, Illinois, and building principal for the Mount Vernon City Schools, District 80. Also, he was an administrator for Danville School District 118 and East St. Louis School District 189. Prior to becoming an administrator, Dr. Rice taught U.S. history for District 189 as well as Springfield Public Schools 186. He is the author of the best-selling books *Vanishing School Boards* and *The Essential Quick Flip Reference Guide for School Board Members*. Due to his educational experience, Dr. Rice has conducted numerous workshops and seminars and is a sought after presenter. A native of East St. Louis, Illinois, Dr. Rice is a noted member of Alpha Phi Alpha Fraternity, Inc. He graduated from Southwestern Illinois College, Eastern Illinois University, and Southern Illinois University at Carbondale and has multiple certifications including his superintendent's endorsement.

Made in the USA
Middletown, DE
07 March 2020